Caleb
Man of faith wh  fully

People ᴵᴺ
THE BIBLE

Robert Dale

DayOne

© Day One Publications 2018

ISBN 978-1-84625-605-9

British Library Cataloguing in Publication Data available

Published by Day One Publications
Ryelands Road, Leominster, HR6 8NZ
Telephone 01568 613 740 FAX 01568 611 473
email—sales@dayone.co.uk
web site—www.dayone.co.uk

Cover design by Kathryn Chedgzoy
Printed by TJ International

To family and friends in the church,
who encouraged me to write this book
after my retirement.

This book on the life and times of Caleb manages the rare feat of being of benefit to both young and mature Christians. A heart-warming read, the book is informative and filled with memorable biblical illustrations which inspire faith and reaffirm that our God is able!

Hugh Hill, retired pastor, Thomas Cooper Memorial Baptist Church, Lincoln

At a time when Christians are increasingly in the minority for their beliefs, the life of Caleb provides a much-needed example of courageous faith. Robert Dale unpacks practical lessons from Caleb's life, for both young and old, with simplicity and a pastor's heart. Short, readable chapters make for an engaging character study, suitable for both individual devotions and small groups.

John Percival, Senior Pastor, Ambassador International Church, Hong Kong

Contents

Joshua the son of Nun
And Caleb the son of Jephunneh
Were the only ones who entered in
To the land of milk and honey.

I heard this little rhyme many years ago from an older Christian who had heard it in Sunday school. It only works, of course, if you pronounce it the English way, 'Jefunny'; it would not work with the Hebrew pronunciation, 'Yeffunay'!

It sums up, however, what was special about Caleb—he reached the Promised Land, whereas thousands did not.

He was not quite unique in this—Joshua got there too. But he was 'semi-unique'—one of only two men out of an entire generation who actually survived the journey from Egypt to Canaan, and saw the fulfilment of God's promise to Israel.

This was not just a matter of natural longevity—outliving his contemporaries, like some brave survivor from the First World War living on into the twenty-first century. It was the reward of faith.

It all hinged on events at Kadesh Barnea, recounted in Numbers 13, when Caleb and Joshua, alone among the twelve spies sent out by Moses, had the faith to believe they could conquer the land. The rest were afraid and discouraged the people, who therefore refused to go in. They were therefore condemned to wander for forty years in the wilderness, and a whole generation died there. Caleb and Joshua alone, God said, would enter in.

But this was not a one-off expression of faith. Caleb showed his faith again, in Joshua 14, when the land was being divided. At the age of eight-five, he demanded, 'Give me this mountain'—a phrase which has become proverbial amongst Christians as an expression of faith-driven ambition.

Caleb is, surprisingly, not mentioned in the great list of 'heroes of faith' in Hebrews 11, but if he were, it might say of him, 'By faith, Caleb entered into the land, whereas the rest of his generation failed to do so. By faith, he took possession of his inheritance, whereas others struggled to do so.' God gave him this testimony, that he had 'a different spirit' and had 'followed [God] fully' (Num. 14:24). He was a man of faith.

Caleb is, however, largely forgotten today, being overshadowed by Joshua. Joshua became the leader of Israel; a whole book is named after him; people sing how 'Joshua fought the battle of Jericho'; but Caleb is usually overlooked.

This short book aims to redress the balance and remind us of a great man of God whose faith is still an example to us today

A slave set free (Exod. 1–12)

We are all, to some extent, the product of our past. The first mention of Caleb is in Numbers 13:6, by which time he is forty. To understand him, however, we need to go back to his earlier experiences. We can do that with Caleb because he was part of a clearly defined group of people, the Israelites, who all went through the same great experience of being brought out of Egypt by the mighty hand of God.

We have, of course, very little personal information about Caleb. We know the name of his father (Jephunneh) and his tribe (Judah), but little else.

There are two Calebs mentioned in the genealogies of 1 Chronicles. Names often occur several times in family histories. My father researched our own family history back to the thirteenth century and found five Thomases and seven Roberts, so two Calebs is not surprising!

Caleb the son of Hezron (1 Chr. 2:18) appears to have been the head of the clan. He was the great-grandson of Judah, and must have lived some time before our Caleb.[1] Various branches of the family are traced, through various wives and concubines, but the direct line to our Caleb is not given. He is, however, mentioned in 1 Chronicles 4:15, along with his sons.

His father is called 'the Kenizzite' in Numbers 32:12. Some have linked this with the Kenezzites of Genesis 15:19, but that seems unlikely, as they were a pagan tribe. It could simply refer to an ancestor called Kenaz.

Regarding Caleb's childhood and early adulthood, there is no information. This is not surprising. The Bible seldom gives us the kinds of details we would expect in a modern biography. Think of Moses, for example: we know he was 'learned in all the wisdom of the Egyptians' (Acts 7:22), and we would love to know more, but any details are left to the imagination of film-makers! Even with Jesus, there is an eighteen-year gap from the age of twelve to the age of thirty. It is not surprising, therefore, that Caleb's childhood is passed over in silence.

That does not mean, however, that we know nothing about his early years. Caleb was an Israelite, and Israel's story was Caleb's story. Caleb was born a little less than forty years before the exodus, when the Israelites were slaves in Egypt. The chart below may help.

80 years before the exodus	Moses born	Exodus 2
40 years before the exodus	Moses flees aged 40	Acts 7:23, 29
Soon after	Caleb born	
THE EXODUS	Moses returns aged 80	Exodus 7:7
	The Israelites leave Egypt	Exodus 12
1 year+ after the exodus	The Israelites leave Sinai	Numbers 10:11–12
Soon after	Caleb sent to spy out the land aged 40	Numbers 13; Joshua 14:7
40 years after the exodus	Moses dies aged 120	Deuteronomy 34:7
Soon after	Caleb 85 years old	Joshua 14:10

Caleb's youth and early manhood, therefore, were lived during some of the darkest days of Israel's history, days of unparalleled suffering.

A people enslaved

The Israelites first went to Egypt to escape the famine in the days of Joseph. At first they were honoured guests, but then 'there arose a new king over Egypt, who did not know Joseph' (Exod. 1:8). Alarmed by all of these 'foreigners', he forced them into slavery. He even tried genocide, ordering all their baby boys to be killed. It failed, of course, and among those who escaped was Moses, rescued, ironically, out of the Nile by Pharaoh's daughter.

The people of Israel have survived many attempts to destroy them. Pharaoh, Haman and Nebuchadnezzar all tried and failed. Most notoriously, Hitler had six million Jews killed in the Holocaust, yet three years later, the State of Israel was declared. Israel has proved to be indestructible.

The same is true of the church—still growing despite endless persecution. As Tertullian said, 'The blood of the martyrs is the seed of the church.'

Even so, these were terrible times for Israel. There was a brief moment of hope when Moses came of age, visited his people, saw their affliction and tried to help. But in a moment of rage he killed an Egyptian; he had to flee the country and all hope was gone.

It was about this time that Caleb was born.

The name Caleb is thought to mean 'dog' (from the Hebrew *kelev*)—a strange name for a child! No reason is given for him being given this name, though he certainly proved 'dogged' in his determination to follow the Lord.[2]

Jephunneh and his wife brought forth their little 'dog' into a world of suffering. They could expect their child to grow up as a slave. Paul could boast, 'I was born free' (Acts 22:28 KJV). Caleb would have to say, 'I was born a slave.'

Israel's only hope lay with the Lord. They must have heard of God's promise to Abraham, to make of him a great nation, in Canaan (Gen. 12:1–5). They may have heard of Abraham's vision of four hundred years of affliction in a strange land (Gen. 15:13–14). One day, surely, God would rescue them.

But no rescue came. Even when Pharaoh died, his successor continued the same policy, so that 'the children of Israel groaned because of the bondage' (Exod. 2:23), Caleb, no doubt, among them.

Millions today are groaning all over the world. At the time of writing, the news is dominated by the civil war in Syria and the famine in South Sudan; we see heart-breaking scenes of people whose lives have been torn apart, including children completely bewildered by it all. Millions elsewhere are also groaning, through famine, war, oppression and even slavery—not to mention all the personal suffering that wears us all down. We live in a groaning world (Rom. 8:22–23). Caleb would have understood that all too well.

Rising above suffering

He was not, however, crushed by it all. Traumatic experiences in childhood can affect people for life, leaving them full of bitterness and doubt, fear and distrust. But not Caleb; he became a strong and confident adult.

Many people do rise above childhood suffering. With some it is simple strength of character. William Pitt the Elder was bullied at school, yet he became one of Britain's greatest Prime Ministers. Andy Murray was at Dunblane Primary School when a gunman shot dead sixteen children and their teacher, yet he became one of the world's greatest tennis players.

With others it is faith. Josiah became king at the age of eight after a disastrous start to life. His father Amon was murdered at the age of twenty-four. Yet 'in the eighth year of his reign, while he was still young, he [Josiah] began to seek ... God' (2 Chr. 34:3). He became one of the greatest kings Judah ever had.

Jesus himself had a traumatic start to life, being born in a stable and fleeing into exile when his life was threatened. Yet he rose above it.

We too can rise above suffering, trusting in a Saviour who rose from the dead. As a pastor, I have known Christians who have suffered terribly in childhood—illness, family breakdown, abuse—and yet rose above it.

We should be gentle and understanding towards those who struggle with the past. If some of the Israelites had doubts about God, we can sympathize. But it is not inevitable that our lives will be ruined by bad experiences, still less that our faith will be destroyed by them. Caleb is proof of that.

Remembering the past

Caleb would never forget Egypt. Indeed, God commanded Israel not to forget: 'Remember that you were a slave in the land of Egypt, and the LORD your God brought you out from there by a mighty hand and by an outstretched arm; therefore the LORD your God commanded you to keep the Sabbath day' (Deut. 5:15; there was no Sabbath for the slaves in Egypt!).

We must never be bound by the past. Paul speaks of 'forgetting those things which are behind and reaching forward to those things which are ahead' (Phil. 3:13). But we must remember where we have come from.

Ye seed of Israel's chosen race, ye ransomed from the fall,
Hail Him who saves you by His grace, and crown Him Lord of all.

Ye Gentile sinners ne'er forget the wormwood and the gall.
Go spread your trophies at His feet and hail Him Lord of all.[3]

An unlikely deliverer

God had not, however, forgotten Israel. 'God heard their groaning' (Exod. 2:24), remembered his covenant—and sent Moses to deliver them.

When Moses reappeared, he must have seemed an unlikely deliverer. It was forty years since he had fled from Egypt; he was now eighty, an old man. To the Egyptians—if they remembered him at all—this man was a traitor and a murderer who had wasted the privilege of a royal upbringing and squandered the advantage of an Egyptian education. To the Israelites, he was at best a failed saviour—the man who ran away. For the last forty years he had been a shepherd in the deserts of Midian. How could this man save them? He had no army, no foreign support. He was alone, apart from his brother, Aaron, who was even older than he was. All he had was the command of God—and a rod.

God had appeared to him in the burning bush and told him to go to Pharaoh and demand, 'Let my people go.' He was to lead them to the 'land flowing with milk and honey' (Exod. 3:6–8). And that rod was the sign of his authority.

God often uses surprising means and surprising people. Jesus himself must have appeared an unlikely Saviour—the humble carpenter's son from Nazareth, dying on a cross. How could this man save us? Yet he did!

Moses met with the elders, told them his plan and showed them his power; and 'the people believed' and 'bowed their heads and worshiped' (Exod. 4:31).

Caleb was one of those who believed that day that this old man from the desert could save them. He may even have been one of the elders: he is named as a 'leader' a short while later (Num. 13:2, 6).

An early test

Their faith was soon tested. Moses and Aaron went to see Pharaoh, but their first interview was not a success. Pharaoh refused to let them go, but, instead, added to their burdens—and the people blamed Moses.

For Caleb, it was an early lesson in how easily the Israelites would give up when the going got tough—a problem he would encounter himself at Kadesh.

Christians too can wilt under pressure. Jesus warns us in the Parable of the Sower of the seed which grows up quickly and yet wilts in the sun—those who believe with joy, but stumble as soon as troubles come.

But Moses did not give in. Why should he, when God was with him?

Many battles have been won 'against the odds'. In 1779, during the War of Independence, the American captain John Paul Jones was confronted by HMS *Serapis*, a fifty-gun frigate. In the face of apparently overwhelming odds, he was invited to surrender, but gave the famous reply, 'Surrender? I have not yet begun to fight!' It was the captain of the *Serapis* who later surrendered.

Pharaoh must have expected Moses to surrender. But Moses could have replied, 'I have not yet begun to fight!' Or, to be more accurate, God had not yet begun to fight. And when God fights for his people, there can be only one result.

God's mighty hand

Exodus chapters 7 to 12 record how God defeated Pharaoh and delivered Israel out of Egypt. Moses repeated his demand; Pharaoh again refused. There followed, therefore, the ten plagues—the Nile turned to blood, the frogs, the lice, the flies, the cattle plague, the boils, the hail, the locusts, the darkness and the death of the firstborn. Pharaoh was told again and again, 'Let my people go,' but again and again he refused, until finally, with Egypt virtually destroyed and his own son dead, he gave in.

Caleb, along with everyone else, must have watched with amazement. Nothing like this had been seen in their lifetime. Here was the most powerful nation in the world being brought to its knees—for their sake. 'If God is for us, who can be against us?' (Rom. 8:31).

They must have been amazed also at the hardness of Pharaoh's heart.

Why did he not give in sooner? There is a deep mystery here. On the one hand, there is the sovereignty of God: God had said that *he* would harden Pharaoh's heart, so that he could show his power (Exod. 7:3). On the other hand, there is human responsibility. The Bible says repeatedly, '*Pharaoh* hardened his heart' (Exod. 8:15, 32; 9:34, emphasis added). Only after the sixth plague is the divine hardening mentioned (Exod. 9:12; 10:1, 20, 27; 14:4).

The Bible solemnly warns us against hardening *our* hearts in Psalm 95, which refers not to Pharaoh, but to the Israelites in the wilderness: 'Today, if you will hear His voice: "Do not harden your hearts, as in the rebellion, as in the day of trial in the wilderness"' (Ps. 95:7–8). Caleb would live to see that day when the Israelites would harden their hearts like Pharaoh, refusing to believe the plain evidence of God's power, refusing to obey the clear commands of God.

But that lay in the future; now was the day of freedom.

Freedom!

William Wordsworth wrote of the French Revolution, 'Bliss was it in that dawn to be alive.'[4] Caleb could have said that about the exodus. It was the greatest event ever in the history of Israel.

It began with the Passover. At twilight, a lamb was to be slain for each household—a perfect lamb in its first year—and the blood sprinkled on the lintels and doorposts. It was to be eaten with unleavened bread and bitter herbs, and the people were to be ready to leave. That night the firstborn of Egypt were slain, but God promised, 'When I see the blood, I will pass over you.'

Caleb would have taken part in this ceremony like everyone else; he may even, as the head of a household, have presided over it in his own home.

He must have wondered what it all meant. Today we know. As Paul says, 'Christ, our Passover, was sacrificed for us' (1 Cor. 5:7). He is the spotless Lamb of God who takes away our sins. Jesus himself made this clear at his final Passover, when he instituted the Lord's Supper, saying, 'This is My body which is given for you ... This ... is ... My blood, which is shed for you' (Luke 22:19–20).

Redemption comes at a price—a price paid by our Lord on the cross, when he offered up himself for the whole household of God.

Could the Israelites have known this? It is possible some did. Jesus says, 'Your father Abraham rejoiced to see My day' (John 8:56); why not, then, the Jews of the exodus? But whether or not they understood it, they observed the ritual; and that night, the tenth plague struck, the firstborn of Egypt were slain, and Pharaoh finally gave in and said, 'Go!' It was freedom at last!

They had been in Egypt 430 years (Exod. 12:41); now at last they were free and on their way to the 'land of milk and honey'.

And Caleb was among them.

NOTES

1   The Talmud, an ancient Jewish commentary, supposes them to be the same, but this cannot be true.

2   Matthew Henry gives an alternative meaning, 'all heart', combining the two Hebrew words kal and lev. If so, that was also prophetic.

3   Edward Perronet and John Rippon, 'All Hail the Power of Jesus' Name'.

4   William Wordsworth, 'The French Revolution as It Appeared to Enthusiasts at Its Commencement', written in 1805.

To the Promised Land— almost! (Exod. 13–Num. 13)

It is actually not very far from Egypt to Canaan. The Promised Land stretched 'from the river of Egypt to the River Euphrates' (Gen. 15:18), so, technically, the moment they crossed the border, they were there! The distance from Cairo to the modern Israeli border, across the Sinai Desert, is about 300 km. In ancient times, there was a major trade route along the coast, the 'Way of the Sea'. A young man like Caleb could walk it in a week or two!

In reality it took rather longer than that. For one thing, we are not talking about a few young men walking at full speed, but 600,000 men of all ages and levels of fitness, together with their families, including young children and elderly people—plus all their flocks, herds and baggage. One cart even included Joseph's bones (Exod. 13:19)! Also, the coastal road went through the land of the Philistines. To avoid war, God therefore led them by a more circuitous route, through the wilderness— via Mount Sinai, to receive the Law.

It was a difficult but thrilling journey—and Caleb was there, every inch of the way. Israel's journey was his journey.

God guiding his people

Caleb would have witnessed many amazing sights on that journey.

Right from the start, 'the LORD went before them by day in a pillar of cloud to lead the way, and by night in a pillar of fire to give them light, so as to go by day and night' (Exod. 13:21). And that cloud remained with them all the way. God was with them, guiding them—and he knew the way!

We also have an infallible guide. Jesus said, 'I am the light of the world' (John 8:12). He guides us by his word and his Spirit—and he knows the way.

The Red Sea

Caleb also witnessed one of the greatest miracles ever seen—the parting of the Red Sea. In Exodus 14, we read how Pharaoh had second thoughts and gathered his army to pursue the Israelites. He caught up with them at the Red Sea. The Israelites were terrified. With the Red Sea before them and Pharaoh's chariots behind them, where could they go?

They ought not to have been surprised. Pharaoh was never going to let them go that easily! And they ought not to have been worried. The same God who had delivered them out of Egypt could also deal with the Egyptian army!

We ought not to be surprised when problems arise. Paul and Barnabas told their new converts: 'We must through many tribulations enter the kingdom of God' (Acts 14:22). The world, the flesh and the devil are all against us. Yet God is with us, and he will bring us *through* all these trials.

God brought the Israelites through this trial—literally! Moses reassured them with these famous words: 'Do not be afraid. Stand still, and see the salvation of the LORD' (Exod. 14:13). Then God said to Moses, 'Tell the children of Israel to go forward. But lift up your rod, and stretch out your hand over the sea and divide it. And the children of Israel shall go on dry ground through the midst of the sea' (14:15–16). And that, of course, was what happened. The waters were parted, the Israelites passed through, and when the Egyptians tried to follow, they were drowned. It was like an eleventh plague, destroying Egypt's army. Israel was delivered and God was glorified.

Caleb was one of those thousands who walked through the Red Sea and sang the Song of Moses: 'I will sing to the LORD, for He has triumphed gloriously! The horse and its rider He has thrown into the sea!' (15:1).

It was a valuable lesson for him that no enemy is too strong for the

Lord and no difficulty too great. If God could overcome the Egyptians, he could certainly overcome the Canaanites. There is nothing too hard for the Lord.

It is a lesson for us, too. In the face of problems, trust in God!

Food, water and war

Caleb saw many more miracles, as God repeatedly showed himself to be a problem-solving God.

First, there were the bitter waters of Marah (Exod. 15:23). No problem: God showed Moses a tree, which made the waters sweet. He then led them on to the beautiful oasis of Elim, with its twelve wells and seventy palm trees—a little foretaste of heaven! Life is not all problems!

Then the people complained that there was nothing to eat (16:2–3). Again, no problem: God sent quails in the evening and manna in the morning.

Again there was a lack of water—this time there was none at all, bitter or sweet (17:1). But again, no problem: God told Moses to strike the rock, and water came out—not just a trickle, but a gushing stream, enough for the whole multitude.

Then they were attacked by the Amalekites (17:8). No problem: Moses lifted up his rod on the hilltop (with support from Aaron and Hur) while Joshua won the battle down below. This has often been taken as a picture of prayer.

Indeed, all these events can be interpreted spiritually. Jesus speaks of himself as the true manna: 'I am the bread of life' (John 6:35). Paul spiritualizes the whole wilderness experience:

Moreover, brethren, I do not want you to be unaware that all our fathers were under the cloud, all passed through the sea, all were baptized into Moses in the cloud and in the sea, all ate the same spiritual food, and all drank the same spiritual drink. For they drank of that spiritual Rock that followed them, and that Rock was Christ. But with most of them God was not well pleased, for their bodies were scattered in the wilderness. (1 Cor. 10:1–5)

We could say of Caleb that he was 'under the cloud, passed through the sea, ate the manna, and drank of the Rock'—only, with him, God *was* pleased.

Israel—and Caleb—had seen, first-hand, God's mighty power to provide and protect. This must have strengthened Caleb's faith in God—though others, it seems, continued to doubt.

Sinai

Next they came to Mount Sinai, where they remained almost a year (Exod. 19:1; Num. 10:11). There, amidst thunder and lightning, fire and darkness, with the mountain quaking and the sound of a trumpet, the Lord gave them the Ten Commandments.

Other laws were also given, and a covenant was made, sealed with blood, in which Israel promised to keep God's Law.

Caleb was there. He heard the voice of God; he gave his assent to the Law, along with all Israel.

Moses then went up onto the mountain for forty days and forty nights, receiving the two stone tablets with the Commandments on them, and instructions about the priests, the sacrifices and the tabernacle.

But then disaster struck. In Moses' absence, the people asked Aaron to make gods for them, and he made them a golden calf (Exod. 32:1–4). How astonishing that they should so soon break the second commandment, and that Aaron should prove so weak! The Lord was angry and threatened to destroy Israel. Moses prayed, and the Lord relented; but when Moses saw the golden calf, he too was angry. He broke the tablets—Israel had broken the Law—destroyed the golden calf, had three thousand executed, and went back up the mountain to receive new tablets.

It was a solemn lesson—for Caleb and for all Israel—of how dangerous it is to disobey God. Even today, though we rejoice in the new covenant, with its wonderful promise of forgiveness, we should always remember the holiness of God. 'Our God is a consuming fire' (Heb. 12:29).

Exodus ends on a happier note. Moses returned down the mountain, his face shining with the glory of God; the people brought their offerings, the tabernacle was made, and it was filled with the glory of God (Exod. 40:34). One of the craftsmen, Bezalel, was related to Caleb (Exod. 31:2; 1 Chr. 2:20).

Further laws were given in Leviticus, along with promises and warnings—prosperity and victory if they obeyed; poverty and defeat if they did not.

Caleb surely took all this to heart.

To the border of the land

The Book of Numbers begins with a census. There were 603,550 men aged twenty and above, excluding the Levites, suggesting a total population of at least 2 million.

The Israelites kept the Passover—a year had passed—and set out again into the wilderness, led by the pillar of cloud (Num. 10:11–12).

But again there was trouble, with more complaints. A fire broke out, which only ceased when Moses prayed.

Then the 'mixed multitude' complained about that 'boring' manna, remembering the fish, the cucumbers, the melons, the leeks, the onions and the garlic in Egypt. The Lord gave them quails—until they came 'out of [their] nostrils' (11:20).

There was also a challenge to Moses' authority from Miriam and Aaron, which resulted in Miriam being struck with leprosy, which only healed when Moses prayed for her. These were all formative experiences for Caleb.

Finally they reached Kadesh Barnea, on the borders of Canaan.

This could—and should—have been 'journey's end'. The Israelites could now have entered the Promised Land. But despite all the wonderful works of God they had seen, they lacked the faith to do so.

Considering how they had behaved so far, that is hardly surprising. It is only surprising that God gave them the opportunity.

As we shall see in the coming chapters, for Israel it was a case of 'so near, and yet so far'. If any of the children were asking that classic children's question, 'Are we nearly there yet?', the answer was 'Yes—and yet, no'.

Israel, as we shall see, failed on this occasion.

But Caleb was different. This would prove to be 'his finest hour'.

Our journey

We must pause here to reflect on our own journey.

Our experience may not be as dramatic as Caleb's, but we all have our own story to tell. As Christians, we have been delivered out of the slavery of sin, we have known the Lord guiding us, protecting us, providing for us, by his Word, through the wilderness of this world. We have also, perhaps, known the Lord's chastising hand upon us when we have gone astray.

How have our experiences affected us? Are we full of faith, like Caleb? Or are we full of doubts and complaints?

By the time he reached Kadesh, Caleb could already look back with gratitude at what God had done for him, and look forward with confidence to what God would yet do. He could have sung from the heart:

Through many dangers, toils and snares I have already come,
'Tis grace has led me safe thus far, and grace will lead me home.[1]

We should be able to say the same.

NOTES

1   John Newton, 'Amazing Grace'.

Caleb the spy (Num. 13:1–25)

What image does the word 'spy' conjure up in your mind? Some might perhaps think of James Bond, 007, licensed to kill, driving his customized Aston Martin, drinking and womanizing—a glamorous though often immoral image! Others might think, more realistically, of MI5 and the CIA, or perhaps the KGB (or the FSB, as it is now called). We might imagine men in raincoats passing notes to each other on park benches, or people listening in to tapped phone calls or analysing hacked emails. We might think of famous spies like Mata Hari, executed in France in 1917 for spying for Germany, or Guy Burgess, who eventually went to live in the Soviet Union.

Caleb is mentioned by name for the first time in Numbers 13—as a spy. But he hardly fits these stereotyped images!

He and eleven other men were sent 'to spy out the land'. This was a one-off mission, however—they were not employed as full-time spies—and the information they were asked to bring back was hardly secret. They were asked to find out what the land was like, and whether the inhabitants were strong or weak, few or many—basic information which anyone could gather by simple observation. We might view them as more like scouts in the Wild West, exploring the land ahead of the army—even, to some extent, like surveyors, mapping out the land, albeit in dangerous conditions.

To some extent, they might have guessed in advance what they would find. The Promised Land was not unknown to the Israelites. Their forefathers had lived there—though admittedly that was four hundred years ago. They must have seen Canaanite traders travelling to Egypt and heard from them what the land was like. And God himself had told them what it was like: 'a land flowing with milk and honey'. To some extent,

God was simply inviting them to go and see for themselves that what he had said about the land was true.

But they were not just collecting information. They were preparing for an invasion, and they needed detailed intelligence concerning all aspects of the land and of the challenge ahead.

These were courageous men. They could easily have come under suspicion. Their lives were at risk. But they were also privileged men—the first Israelites to see the Promised Land they were all longing for.

Twelve good men and true?

The story of the twelve spies is told in Numbers 13.

The Israelites were encamped in the Wilderness of Paran—more precisely, at Kadesh (Num. 13:26), also called Kadesh Barnea (Num. 32:8; Deut. 1:19; 9:23; Josh. 14:6). According to Deuteronomy 1:2, this was eleven days' journey from Mount Sinai, though it evidently took them longer.

According to Numbers, the Lord himself gave the command to send out the spies: 'And the LORD spoke to Moses, saying, "Send men to spy out the land of Canaan, which I am giving to the children of Israel: from each tribe of their fathers you shall send a man, every one a leader among them"' (Num. 13:1–2). Moses puts a slightly different slant on it, however, thirty-eight years later on the Plains of Moab, when recalling what had happened:

So we departed from Horeb, and went through all that great and terrible wilderness … Then we came to Kadesh Barnea. And I said to you, 'You have come to the mountains of the Amorites, which the LORD our God is giving us. Look, the LORD your God has set the land before you; go up and possess it, as the LORD God of your fathers has spoken to you; do not fear or be discouraged.

And every one of you came near to me and said, 'Let us send men before us, and let them search out the land for us, and bring back word to us of the way by which we should go up, and of the cities into which we shall come.'

This plan pleased me well; so I took twelve of your men, one man from each tribe. (Deut. 1:19–23)

Matthew Henry detects unbelief here—the people wanting to see for themselves, rather than simply trusting the Lord.[1] However, Moses says 'the plan pleased me well', and the Lord does not say he is displeased with it. There is no contradiction between God commanding it and the people suggesting it: God often adds his seal to human ideas—the advice of our friends or family, for example, or the wisdom of our church leaders.

No doubts are expressed at this stage. The people are not questioning *whether* they should 'go up', simply *how*. And the Lord's command should remove any doubts. There is an implied promise of success when he says he is *giving* them this land. Victory is assured. Whilst useful as a reconnaissance trip, this is really just a preview, to encourage them—though God also intends to test their faith by showing them the problems.

The twelve men are listed by name:

From Reuben, Shammua, the son of Zaccur

From Simeon, Shaphat, the son of Hori

From Judah, Caleb, the son of Jephunneh

From Issachar, Igal, the son of Joseph

From Ephraim, Hoshea (Joshua), the son of Nun

From Benjamin, Palti, the son of Raphu

From Zebulun, Gaddiel, the son of Sodi

From Manasseh, Gaddi, the son of Susi

From Dan, Ammiel, the son of Gemalli

From Asher, Sethur, the son of Michael

Chapter 3

From Naphtali, Nahbi, the son of Vophsi
From Gad, Geuel, the son of Machi.

No one was sent from the tribe of Levi, as they were set apart for the service of God in the tabernacle.

Now, here is a challenge for you: How many of these names did you know, apart from Joshua and Caleb? If you want a difficult question for a Bible quiz, ask people to name, from memory, *any* of the other ten spies. These men have disappeared into dishonourable oblivion! Only the men of faith are remembered. That is true, generally, in church history. A few 'arch villains' are remembered, but, for the most part, we remember only the 'heroes of faith'. If we wish to be remembered ourselves, let it be for our faith!

These twelve men were, however, all leaders of their tribes, and to them a very responsible task was given. The rest of Israel had not yet seen the land; their impressions of it would depend on the word of these twelve men.

We might compare them with a modern jury—'twelve good men and true'—who have the solemn responsibility of deciding whether the defendant is innocent or guilty. These twelve men were invited to decide whether the land was good or bad. The Lord had given his testimony: he had told them it was good. He was inviting them now to look at the evidence. Would they prove to be a reliable jury?

We may perhaps think of another twelve men, chosen by our Lord Jesus Christ—the twelve apostles, sent out in Matthew 10 into that same land of Israel, and later into all the world. They were not leaders of their tribes—they were mostly simple, uneducated men—and yet the Lord entrusted them with the preaching of the gospel. They had the privilege of knowing Jesus and being taught by him. What the world thought of Jesus would depend, to a large degree, on what they said of him. We today are dependent on their reports, written in the Gospels. Thankfully only one of them, Judas, failed in his duty; the others, by the grace of God, all turned out to be 'good men and true'.

Christians today have inherited that responsibility, to bring to the world a 'good report' of our Lord Jesus Christ, of the Christian life, and of the Christian hope of the world to come. True, ultimately it is not our words but the Spirit of God who leads people to salvation, but our words can either encourage or discourage people in seeking the Lord. How faithful are we in this responsibility?

Spy out the land

Moses gives his instructions in Numbers 13:17–20, telling them to consider both the people and the land:

Then Moses sent them to spy out the land of Canaan, and said to them, 'Go up this way into the South, and go up to the mountains, and see what the land is like: *whether* the people who dwell in it are strong or weak, few or many; *whether* the land they dwell in is good or bad; *whether* the cities they inhabit are like camps or strongholds; *whether* the land is rich or poor; and *whether* there are forests there or not. Be of good courage. And bring some of the fruit of the land' [emphasis added].

There are five 'whether's here, or six if you count the first as two questions. The correct answers should have been: strong (but not too strong), many (but not too many), good (a land of milk and honey), strongholds (but not impregnable), rich (wonderfully rich), and yes (in contrast with the desert)—a good land, ready to be conquered.

Significantly, they were *not* asked to say *whether* it could be conquered or not. That 'whether' was not on the list, because there was no 'whether' about it—the Lord had already told them that he was *giving* them this land.

The final requirement, to bring some of the fruit of the land, is intriguing. The idea was to bring proof that the land really was as good as

God had said it was. God, in his sovereignty, had ordered events so that there would be something impressive to bring back: it was 'the season of the first ripe grapes' (Num. 13:20). If they had gone in winter, they might have had difficulty finding anything, but God had sent them there at harvest time.

The 'fruit of the land' features also in the story of Joseph. When his brothers came to buy grain in Egypt, Joseph accused them of being spies, and sent them home to fetch Benjamin. Their father Jacob reluctantly agreed, but told them to go with a gift: 'Take some of the best fruits of the land in your vessels and carry down a present for the man—a little balm and a little honey, spices and myrrh, pistachio nuts and almonds' (Gen. 43:11). Even in a time of famine, Israel could yield such riches. Perhaps Joseph, seeing these fruits, thought longingly of his own land, the land which, even then, God had promised to his people.

These fruits that the spies were to bring back were intended to stir up a longing in the people of Israel to be in that land.

Is there any equivalent in our lives to this 'spying out the land'?

Of course there is. Every time we read the Bible, we are 'spying out the land'—exploring the riches of our spiritual inheritance, both here in this life and in the world to come, the 'land' God has given us in Christ, along with all the challenges involved.

And we do have some of the fruit of the land to carry home with us. Forgiveness of sin, fellowship with God, the fruit of the Spirit—these are all tokens of the glory of heaven. Paul calls the Spirit 'the guarantee of our inheritance' (Eph. 1:14). The land God has given us is a good land!

Mission accomplished

The spies duly went and explored the land 'from the Wilderness of Zin as far as Rehob, near the entrance of Hamath' (Num. 13:21)—from the far south to the far north, a distance of about 400 km each way, which took them forty days (v. 25). Whether they stayed together the whole time, or whether they travelled separately (or perhaps two by two, like the apostles), we are not told.

Special mention is made of their visit to Hebron in the south, where they saw the descendants of Anak—Ahiman, Sheshai and Talmai (v. 22). Both the city and its inhabitants made an impression on them. Hebron, we are told, was a very ancient city, seven years older than Zoan in Egypt (v. 22)—Zoan being the royal residence of Pharaoh, where Moses had performed his miracles (Ps. 78:12)—and its inhabitants were 'giants' (v. 33). It was this that struck fear into the hearts of the ten unfaithful spies.

Hebron was also the home of Abraham (Gen. 13:18) and later his burial place, along with that of Sarah, Isaac, Rebekah, Leah and Jacob (Gen. 23:19; 25:8–10; 49:29–31). It is still a holy place for the Jews to this day (and indeed for Muslims, who regard the patriarchs as prophets). Whether the spies saw the tomb we are not told; we can only imagine what feelings it would have inspired if they did, to see the burial place of their ancestors, those to whom the original promise of the land had been given, and to know that those ancient promises were about to be fulfilled. That tomb was the only land Abraham ever owned in Canaan; soon the whole land would be theirs. Caleb in particular must have been deeply impressed by Hebron, as he later claimed it as his inheritance (Josh. 14:13).

Having seen all this, the spies also brought back some of the fruit of the land, as commanded: 'Then they came to the Valley of Eshcol, and there cut down a branch with one cluster of grapes; they carried it between two of them on a pole. They also brought some of the pomegranates and figs' (Num. 13:23). Eshcol is thought to be the valley north of Hebron; the name means 'cluster'. That branch must have been quite impressive, requiring two men to carry it.

Israel is still noted for its vineyards today, and there is a thriving wine industry, though it is mainly concentrated in the north. The modern Israeli wine industry was founded by Baron Rothschild, of Château

Lafite fame, and wine exports currently exceed $40 million. There are still vineyards near Hebron (which today is within the Palestinian territories). Hevron Heights Winery produces the intriguingly named Elone Mamre Chardonnay, which is highly rated by some wine experts.

That cluster of grapes proclaimed loudly, 'This is a *good* land!' It was also, as Matthew Henry puts it, 'an earnest of good things to come'.

There is also a symbolic meaning in all this, which is still relevant today. The vine is one of the symbols of Israel in the Bible (Ps. 80:8; Isa. 5:1). This may lie behind our Lord's choice of imagery in John 15, where he says, 'I am the vine, you are the branches' (v. 5). He goes on to say, 'By this My is Father glorified, that you bear much fruit' (v. 8). We could take these grapes of Eshcol as a symbol of the fruitfulness that God looks for in us—not just the odd shrivelled grape, but a great cluster of grapes: *much* fruit.

After forty days, then, the spies returned to the camp.

In retrospect, it is amazing that they survived unscathed. One could easily imagine them being challenged, especially carrying that large cluster of grapes. Perhaps, since it was harvest time, there were others carrying grapes, but one could imagine someone asking them: 'Where are you going with that?' Whether people noticed them or not, however, they went unharmed: the sovereign God was protecting them, as he protects us today.

That in itself should have spoken to them of God's power to fulfil his promises. God had protected them; he could surely protect the whole nation.

The mission had been a success. The report, however, was a disaster.

NOTES

1   Matthew Henry, *Commentary on the Whole Bible*, on Numbers 13.

Fear and faith (Num. 13:26–33)

In December 1862, during the American Civil War, President Abraham Lincoln said in his annual Message to Congress:

Fellow-citizens, we cannot escape history. We of this Congress and this administration, will be remembered in spite of ourselves. No personal significance, or insignificance, can spare one or another of us. The fiery trial through which we pass, will light us down, in honor or dishonor, to the latest generation.[1]

Similar words could have been spoken of the twelve spies and of the Israelites at Kadesh Barnea. This was their moment of truth which would 'light them down, in honour or dishonour', to all generations.

Reporting the facts

It began well enough. The twelve spies returned 'to Moses and Aaron and all the congregation' and gave their report:

They brought back word to them and to all the congregation, and showed them the fruit of the land. Then they told him [Moses], and said, 'We went to the land where you sent us. It truly flows with milk and honey, and this is its fruit. Nevertheless the people who dwell in the land are strong; the cities are fortified and very large; moreover we saw the descendants of Anak there. The Amalekites dwell in the land of the South; the Hittites, the Jebusites, and the Amorites dwell in the mountains; and the Canaanites dwell by the sea and along the banks of the Jordan.' (Num. 13:26–29)

We are not told who the spokesman was or whether all twelve chipped in. We might imagine Joshua and Caleb giving the positive side and the others the negative, but the whole report is attributed to the twelve collectively.

And all that they said was true. This was a fair and honest summary of what they had seen: it *was* a good land, a land of milk and honey, just as they had been promised, but there *were* challenges ahead: the people *were* strong, the cities *were* fortified, and there *were* 'giants' to contend with.

This was no surprise. The Canaanites had been there since the days of Abraham (Gen. 12:6), and God had called it 'the land of the Canaanites and the Hittites and the Amorites and the Perizzites and the Hivites and the Jebusites … a land flowing with milk and honey' (Exod. 3:17). The report merely confirmed this, with a little more detail about the location and strength of these tribes, and the richness of the land. They knew about the milk and honey; grapes, pomegranates and figs were a bonus! The message was simple: it was a good land, but there were challenges ahead—exactly as God had said.

A similar report could be given—and is given in the New Testament—of the Christian life. It is a good life, but there are challenges. We are promised heaven, but the way is hard. Jesus himself was honest about this:

Narrow is the gate and difficult is the way which leads to life, and there are few who find it. (Matt. 7:14)

Whoever does not bear his cross and come after Me cannot be My disciple. For which of you, intending to build a tower, does not sit down first and count the cost, whether he has enough to finish it …? Or what king, going to make war against another king, does not sit down first and consider whether he is able with ten thousand to meet him who comes against him with twenty thousand? (Luke 14:27–31)

The Christian life is not easy. The world, the flesh and the devil are against us. Faithful preachers and writers have always taught this.

John Bunyan, for example, in his *Pilgrim's Progress*, describes some wonderful experiences—Christian's burden rolling away at Calvary, the Interpreter's House, the Palace Beautiful, the Delectable Mountains— and the end is glorious: the Heavenly City. But there are many challenges—the Slough of Despond, the Hill Difficulty, Vanity Fair, Giant Despair, the Valley of the Shadow of Death, not to mention the crossing of the river at the end.

However, in the face of all these difficulties, faith says: 'If God is for us, who can be against us? … In all these things we are more than conquerors through Him who loved us' (Rom. 8:31, 37).

Faith does not mean glossing over the challenges, but facing up to them confidently in Christ. It would have been both dishonest and unhelpful if the spies had not mentioned the difficulties ahead. The Israelites were not to be led into Canaan under false pretences. They must not go in unprepared. They needed to know the facts. And people today need to know the facts about the Christian life. A 'gospel' which makes it all sound easy is a false gospel.

The question, however, is what will we do with those facts?

The faith of Caleb

This was Caleb's moment. Seeing the agitation of the crowd, Caleb stepped forward to reassure and encourage them: 'Then Caleb quieted the people before Moses, and said, "Let us go up at once and take possession, for we are well able to overcome it"' (Num. 13:30).

Caleb here is like an Old Testament Barnabas—a 'Son of Encouragement' and a man 'full … of faith' (Acts 4:36; 11:24). Indeed the comparison becomes stronger as the story continues. Joshua and Caleb are mentioned together here, like Paul and Barnabas, but Caleb later fades into the background, like Barnabas, while Joshua becomes the leader, like Paul.

Caleb was quite confident they could conquer Canaan—and of course he had every reason to be confident.

Caleb was now forty years old (so he tells us later in Josh. 14:7), and everything he had seen in the last forty years would have led him to be confident in God and eager to go in to the land.

Remembering the slavery of his youth, he would have longed for the land of freedom. Remembering the hardships of the wilderness, he would have wanted to be in the land of milk and honey. Seeing that land for himself would have proved to him that God's word was true. Remembering the plagues that God had brought upon Egypt, that amazing deliverance of the night of the Passover, the parting of the Red Sea and the drowning of the Egyptian army would have convinced him of God's power. If the Egyptian army—the greatest army in the world—was unable to stand against God, why should the Israelites be afraid of a few oversized Canaanites? They had defeated the Amalekites also; surely they were 'well able' to overcome the Canaanites. All the other miracles—the cloud, the manna, the water and the quails—would have strengthened his faith. The mountain had quaked at the presence of God at Sinai. How could they doubt that this God would give them the victory? Indeed, Caleb does not speak of 'conquering' the land; since God had given it to them, he speaks merely of 'possessing' it. He could have said with Mary:

He who is mighty has done great things for me,
And holy is His name …
He has shown strength with His arm;
He has scattered the proud in the imagination of their hearts.
He has put down the mighty from their thrones,
And exalted the lowly. (Luke 1:49–52)

Caleb would fully expect God to 'help His servant Israel' and fulfil his promise to Abraham by giving them the land (Luke 1:54–55).

In short, he believed God's word, having ample evidence to convince him of God's faithfulness and power.

We today have even more reason to believe. Of course, ideally, we should believe God's word even without any evidence. But God, in his goodness, has given us ample evidence to convince us.

We have the evidence of creation. As Paul says, 'Since the creation of the world [God's] invisible attributes are clearly seen, being understood by the things that are made, even His eternal power and Godhead, so that they are without excuse' (Rom. 1:20).

We have the evidence of providence. Paul again: 'He did not leave Himself without witness, in that He did good, gave us rain from heaven and fruitful seasons, filling our hearts with food and gladness' (Acts 14:17).

We have Old Testament history—including the account of the exodus. Those 'heroes of faith' in Hebrews 11 are all saying to us, 'You can trust in God.'

We have the whole story of Christ fulfilling a whole host of prophecies. Christ was the promised descendant of Abraham through whom the world would be blessed, the promised descendant of David who would rule the world, the promised Lamb who would take away the sin of the world. God keeps his word: he has sent his Son as he said he would! And having died as prophesied, Christ has risen again, having shown himself alive 'by many infallible proofs' (Acts 1:3).

We have the coming of the Spirit and the miracles of the apostles, all testifying to us that the gospel is true.

We have the evidence of history—the growth of the church over two thousand years despite every effort to destroy it.

We have the evidence of our own experience—God has changed our lives, given us a new heart, filled us with his Spirit, answered our prayers, and helped us in all kinds of remarkable ways.

All this should convince us that we can trust in God!

We all have our Kadesh Barnea moments, when we stand on the brink of some new enterprise and we have to decide, 'Can I do it?' Perhaps it is a new job, or some new work in the church, or a call to the mission field. Can we do it? Faith says that if it is God's will, we can. Jesus says, 'All things are possible to him who believes' (Mark 9:23). Paul says, 'I can do all things through Christ who strengthens me' (Phil. 4:13).

Caleb certainly believed that—and Joshua agreed with him, to judge from his subsequent support in Numbers 14. But the others were not so sure.

The fear of the rest

The others immediately raised objections and flatly contradicted Caleb, saying, 'We are not able to go up against the people, for they are stronger than we' (Num. 13:31). Even if that were true, it was not the point. Whatever the strength of the two armies, God was with the Israelites and he had promised them the land. That was enough. As the saying goes, 'One plus God is a majority.'

Then an extraordinary thing happened. The ten spies began to lie and to contradict their earlier report—or at least, to put a negative 'spin' on it:

And they gave the children of Israel a bad report of the land which they had spied out, saying, 'The land through which we have gone as spies is a land that devours its inhabitants, and all the people whom we saw in it are men of great stature. There we saw the giants (the descendants of Anak came from the giants); and we were like grasshoppers in our own sight, and so we were in their sight. (Num. 13:32–33)

How many twisted facts can we count up here?

To begin with, how could they say it was a land that 'devoured its inhabitants' when they had just said it was a land of milk and honey and when they had just shown them that cluster of grapes? It was obviously not true.

Then again, was it really true that *all* the men were of great stature? Some undoubtedly were, but surely not *all*? And how big a problem (so to speak!) were those 'giants'? Verse 22 lists three 'descendants of Anak' in Hebron. They evidently did not trouble the spies too much at the time, as they went on to the Valley of Eshcol nearby and collected their grapes. Now they are called 'giants'[2] and are regarded as a reason for not going into Canaan.

And what about that comparison with grasshoppers? Very poetic, but again, an exaggeration. God says in Isaiah 40:22 that the inhabitants of the earth are like grasshoppers before *him*. Were the Israelites suggesting that these Anakim were like gods?

This report was so twisted, it was a false report—and the Law said specifically, 'You shall not circulate a false report' (Exod. 23:1).

We need not doubt that there were 'giants' in the land. We are not in the realms of fairy tales here. The Bible mentions several giants. Later on in their journey, the Israelites encountered, and defeated, Og the king of Bashan, whose bedstead was nine cubits long (Deut. 3:11). There was the 'giant' Goliath, who was slain by David. He was 'six cubits and a span'—about 3 metres (1 Sam. 17:4). There were also four sons of 'the giant in Gath' who fell 'by the hand of David and ... his servants' (2 Sam. 21:19–22). These men were prodigies and were regarded with fear, but, in the end, they were no match for Israelite warriors with God on their side.

It may even be that the Canaanites were generally taller than the Israelites. Some nationalities today are taller than others. The average height of men in England is 1.75 metres, compared with 1.67 metres in China (very useful in a crowd, as I found out recently at a Chinese New Year Parade!). But I am sure the Chinese are not afraid of the English because of that!

The ten spies, however, seemed to be overawed by these sons of Anak, and by the Canaanites generally. The truth is, they had been overcome by fear, and fear does strange things to our perception of the facts.

There is an interesting example of this in the story of Cabeza de Vaca, a Spanish explorer in the sixteenth century. Having been shipwrecked on the Florida coast, he and a handful of companions made their way, amidst great hardships, around the Gulf of Mexico. He later wrote that on encountering 'about a hundred Indian archers ... our fear was so great, that, whether they were tall or short, they seemed like giants to us'.[3]

These spies were overwhelmed by fear. They had seen the problems, and they seemed huge in their eyes. They had lost sight of God—they could see only the difficulties. They imagined the conquest of Canaan to be impossible, and wanted to stop Israel from even trying. They had been told by Moses, 'Be of good courage' (v. 20) and they had been courageous, going through the land; but now their courage had failed, and they were full of fear.

Even from a human viewpoint, this was an extraordinary loss of nerve. Israel had, after all, 600,000 men able to go to war! But in view of God's promises and power, it was inexcusable.

There are times, if we are honest, when we are overcome with fear.

Fear is like fog, which hides God from view but makes every obstacle look larger than it is. We see the giants, we feel like grasshoppers, and we forget altogether the greatness of God. We become fixated on the problems and end up attempting nothing, when all along God is saying to us, 'Fear not!' That phrase 'Fear not' (or some similar phrase) occurs over a hundred times in the Bible—because God knows what we are like, and that we need constant reassurance.

At the root of it all, however, is unbelief.

God says to Moses later, 'How long will these people ... not believe Me ...?' (Num. 14:11). That was true of the spies also: they had not *believed* God's word; and whereas faith produces courage, unbelief engenders fear.

There is a striking story of faith, fear and unbelief in the New Testament, when Peter walks on water (Matt. 14:22–33). After the feeding of the five thousand, the disciples set out across the Sea of Galilee, while Jesus goes up onto the mountain alone. Seeing them struggling in the middle of the night, Jesus comes walking on the water. 'It is I,' he says; 'do not be afraid.' Peter, full of faith, asks to walk on the water, and for a few amazing moments he does so. But then fear sets in: seeing the wind, he begins to sink. He cries out for help, and Jesus graciously saves him. Even so, Jesus rebukes him—not for his fear, but for his doubt: 'O you of little faith, why did you doubt?'

That is the problem here. Of course, no one actually says, 'I don't believe God's promise.' But that is the unspoken problem at the root of it all.

Why the difference?

There is a deep mystery here.

Why did Caleb and Joshua believe, while the others were afraid? Surely they had all been through the same experiences? They had all seen the mighty hand of God delivering them out of Egypt. They had all 'passed through the Sea'. They had all experienced the Lord's faithfulness in the wilderness. They had all seen the same sights in Canaan. It was not as if Caleb had gone to a peaceful valley in the north while the others alone had seen the giants in the south. Why did two react with faith, but the other ten with unbelief? Was it simply a difference of character, or was there something deeper?

The New Testament answers that faith is the gift of God (Eph. 2:8). That does not give us an excuse for unbelief: we *ought* to believe God's word, and the evidence should lead us to believe. But in our fallen condition, we are blind until God opens our eyes to see the truth. That is why, today, two people can listen to the same sermon, and one is converted and the other unmoved. That is why, if we *have* believed, we ought not to boast, but to give thanks to God.

The responsibility however, remains ours—God requires us to believe, and there is every reason to believe. If we believe, the rewards are wonderful; if we do not, the results are disastrous.

The twelve spies are divided—two full of faith, ten full of fear. Now the people must make their choice.

NOTES

1 'Annual Message to Congress: Concluding Remarks', Abraham Lincoln Online, http://www.abrahamlincolnonline.org/lincoln/speeches/congress.htm.

2 The same Hebrew word, *Nephilim*, is used of the giants in Genesis 6:4.

3 Cabeza de Vaca, *The Shipwrecked Men* (London: Penguin, 2007), p. 42. They turned out to be friendly!

Standing alone (Num. 14:1–10)

Ancient Israel was not a democracy. At no point did Moses offer the people a vote on whether to go into Canaan or not. Israel was a theocracy. God was their King, with Moses as his representative. They were expected to obey Moses, following whatever commands God gave him.

However, even the greatest leader needs the agreement of the people. Even the best shepherd can do nothing if the sheep will not follow. Only Christ could say categorically, 'My sheep hear My voice … and they follow Me' (John 10:27)—and we only follow *him* reluctantly at times!

Israel did not follow their leader at Kadesh Barnea. Having heard, in effect, two different reports—a 'minority report' from Caleb (and Joshua), advising them to go into Canaan at once, and a 'majority report' from the others, saying not to go—they followed the majority. Faced with a choice between faith and fear, they chose fear. And that fear turned rapidly into outright rebellion.

Spiralling rebellion

Their reaction went far beyond anything the ten spies had said.

They 'lifted up their voices and cried, and … wept that night' (Num. 14:1). They complained against Moses and Aaron (the KJV has the evocative word 'murmured'). They wished they had died in Egypt, or in the wilderness. They began to think hard thoughts against God: 'Why has the LORD brought us to this land to fall by the sword, that our wives and children should become victims?' Finally they talked of outright rebellion: 'Let us select a leader and return to Egypt' (14:1–4). Instead of going forwards, they wanted to go backwards.

Years later, Moses gives this graphic description:

You would not go up, but rebelled against the command of the LORD your God; and you complained in your tents, and said, 'Because the LORD hates us, He has brought us out of the land of Egypt to deliver us into the hand of the Amorites, to destroy us. Where can we go up? Our brethren have discouraged our hearts, saying, 'The people are greater and taller than we; the cities are great and fortified up to heaven; moreover we have seen the sons of the Anakim there.' (Deut. 1:26–28)

Discouragement often spirals out of control, causing demoralization and rebellion. The ten spies might say they had only counselled caution, but they had set in motion a train of events that could have destroyed the whole nation.

This is also true in the church. It is right sometimes to counsel caution, and it is not necessary to be constantly upbeat. We have to be truthful, recognize genuine difficulties and talk them through. But gloomy words can be discouraging, with effects out of all proportion to anything we intended—whereas encouraging words can spread optimism and hope, and awaken faith.

We live in an age when we are encouraged to be open and express our feelings. But sometimes it is best to hold back our thoughts. In Psalm 73, the psalmist had been struggling with dark thoughts. But he kept this to himself: 'If I had said, "I will speak thus," behold I would have been untrue to the generation of Your children' (Ps. 73:15). Then he went into the sanctuary, and it all became clear.

If only the ten spies had kept their fears to themselves! It was understandable that they should have had dark thoughts as they saw those 'giants', and that doubts entered their minds—all of us are prey to doubts. The real sin was giving way to those doubts and blurting them out. If only they had paused and prayed—and talked with Caleb—it might all have been different.

There was a famous poster in the Second World War: 'Careless talk costs lives.' Its aim was not only to prevent sensitive information getting into enemy hands, but also to keep demoralizing rumours from spreading. The report of the ten spies could be described as 'careless talk' and it did literally cost lives.

The blame cannot be put entirely on the ten spies, however. The people overreacted, and God held them accountable in the judgement that followed. It was not, 'How long will these spies reject Me?' but 'How long will these *people* reject Me?' (Num. 14:11). We are all accountable for our own decisions.

Pleading with the people

Confronted with this rebellion, Moses and Aaron 'fell on their faces before all the assembly' (14:5), whilst Joshua and Caleb 'tore their clothes' (v. 6).

Tearing one's clothes was a common cultural expression of grief and anger in ancient times. Examples include Reuben when Joseph was sold (Gen. 37:29), Jacob when he saw Joseph's bloodstained tunic (Gen. 37:34), Josiah when he heard the Law (2 Chr. 34:19) and Job when he was told his children were dead (Job 1:20). The high priest Caiaphas tore his clothes at the supposed 'blasphemy' of Jesus claiming to be the Son of God (Matt. 26:65)—though this was forbidden in the Law (Lev. 10:6; 21:10). Paul and Barnabas tore their clothes when they were treated as gods (Acts 14:14)—another similarity with Joshua and Caleb, tearing their clothes in horror at the way the people were behaving, though for rather different reasons!

Joshua and Caleb were clearly distraught. They knew from past experience how serious this was. They had seen the plagues in Egypt and God's judgements in the wilderness. 'It is a fearful thing to fall into the hands of the living God' (Heb. 10:31). They cared passionately about Israel, and could see judgement coming upon them.

We might not tear our clothes, but we ought surely to care passionately about our national sins today—the greed, the selfishness, the contempt for God and his Law, and the rejection of Christ and his church.

Joshua and Caleb now pleaded with the people:

> The land we passed through … is an exceedingly good land. If the LORD delights in us, then He will bring us into this land and give it to us, 'a land which flows with milk and honey'. Only do not rebel against the LORD, nor fear the people of the land, for they are our bread; their protection has departed from them, and the LORD is with us. Do not fear them. (Num. 14:7–9)

In chapter 13, Caleb was the spokesman. Now it is Joshua and Caleb. It is interesting to see these two standing together. In the list of spies, Joshua was the representative from Ephraim and Caleb the representative from Judah; these two tribes were later the two leading tribes in the north and south respectively. More important in the present context, Joshua was Moses' assistant (Exod. 24:13), and his voice ought therefore to have carried added authority.

Moses said later that he also joined in:

> Then I said to you, 'Do not be terrified, or afraid of them. The LORD your God, who goes before you, He will fight for you, according to all He did for you in Egypt before your eyes, and in the wilderness where you saw how the LORD your God carried you, as a man carries his son, in all the way that you went until you came to this place.' (Deut. 1:29–31)

These are beautiful, powerful, well-reasoned speeches from godly men—men of authority who ought to be listened to. Remember what God has done for you, they are saying; remember his promises: you can trust in him.

Yet the people did not listen. No amount of eloquence could persuade them, no amount of truth could convince them, even though it came with the combined authority of Moses, Joshua and Caleb.

An evil heart of unbelief

The root of the problem was unbelief. God said so, in Numbers 14:11: 'How long will these people reject Me? And how long will they not believe Me, with all the signs which I have performed among them?' And Moses underlined that in Deuteronomy 1:32–33: 'Yet, for all that, you did not believe the LORD your God, who went in the way before you to search out a place for you to pitch your tents, to show you the way you should go, in the fire by night and in the cloud by day.'

There are several sins here: unreasonableness ('for all that'), rebellion (against the Lord) and ingratitude (after all he had done for them). But at the heart of it all was unbelief ('you did not believe')—and persistent unbelief at that: 'How *long* will they not believe Me?' (emphasis added).

Most people, if asked to name a few sins (supposing they accept the concept of sin at all), will suggest murder, adultery, theft, and the like. They will not generally think of unbelief as a sin. Even Christians sometimes fail to recognize the seriousness of unbelief. Yet Jesus himself identifies it as a sin: 'He [the Holy Spirit] will convict the world of sin, and of righteousness, and of judgment: of sin, because they do not believe in Me' (John 16:8–9).

The Israelites at Kadesh were guilty of unbelief, just like the ten spies. They were quite willing to believe the ten spies, with their twisted report; quite willing to believe the rumour-mongers who said that God hated them. But they were not willing to believe Moses, the servant of God, who had faithfully led them and worked miracles among them, nor Joshua and Caleb, who told them the truth. They were not willing to believe the promises of God. They preferred their own thoughts, and their own fears, to the word of God.

This was a problem of the heart, and it can affect us also. Both the Old and the New Testaments warn us of this:

Today, if you will hear His voice [the voice of the Lord, the great Shepherd of the sheep],
'Do not harden your hearts, as in the rebellion,
As in the day of trial in the wilderness.' (Ps. 95:7–8)

Beware, brethren, lest there be in any of you an evil heart of unbelief in departing from the living God. (Heb. 3:12, commenting on Ps. 95)

Hebrews urges us therefore to 'exhort one another daily'—in other words, to be Calebs and Barnabases, encouraging one another in our faith.

Stone the messenger

That 'evil heart of unbelief' now broke out in violent rebellion, and the lives of Joshua and Caleb (and probably Moses) were suddenly under threat: 'All the congregation said to stone them with stones' (Num. 14:10).

Stoning was the normal method of execution in Israel for the most serious crimes—human sacrifice (Lev. 20:2), mediums (Lev. 20:27), blasphemers (Lev. 24:16), Sabbath-breakers (Num. 15:35), false prophets (Deut. 13:10), idolaters (Deut. 17:5) and, rather alarmingly, disobedient sons (Deut. 21:21—but contrast the Parable of the Prodigal Son) and adulterers (Deut. 22:24—but contrast John 8:1–11). Joshua and Caleb might justly have asked, 'For which of these sins do you take up stones against us?' Perhaps the people really did regard them as false prophets—though actually they were the true prophets.

We have an expression 'to stone the messenger', meaning to silence someone who comes to you with unwelcome news. Joshua and Caleb had come to them with good news, and yet the people talked of stoning them.

This is not the only time in the Bible that God's servants are either stoned or threatened with stoning. When the people complained about the lack of water, Moses said, 'They are almost ready to stone me!' (Exod. 17:4). Jezebel had Naboth stoned, to obtain his vineyard for Ahab (1 Kings 21:9–10). Joash had the prophet Zechariah, the son of Jehoida the priest (who had protected and advised him earlier in his life), stoned in the court of the temple, because he dared to speak the truth about Judah's sins (2 Chr. 24:20–21).

Jesus probably had this in mind in his famous lament over Jerusalem:

Therefore, indeed, I send you prophets, wise men, and scribes: some of them you will kill and crucify, and some of them you will scourge in your synagogues and persecute from city to city, that on you may come all the righteous blood shed on the earth, from the blood of righteous Abel to the blood of Zechariah, son of Berechiah, whom you murdered between the temple and the altar … O Jerusalem, Jerusalem, the one who kills the prophets and stones those who are sent to her! How often I wanted to gather your children together, as a hen gathers her chicks under her wings, but you were not willing! (Matt. 23:34–37)

The second book of Chronicles was the last book of the Hebrew Bible. Abel to Zechariah is, therefore, not only fortuitously A to Z in English, but 'from beginning to end'.

Jesus himself was threatened with stoning in John 10:31 after the Good Shepherd speech—'for blasphemy', they said, 'because You, being a Man, make Yourself God', Jesus having said, 'I and My Father are one' (10:30–33).

Stephen was stoned to death (Acts 7:59). Paul was threatened with stoning at Iconium (Acts 14:5) and left for dead after actually being stoned at Lystra (Acts 14:19)—though he later recovered. He listed this among his many sufferings: 'once I was stoned' (2 Cor. 11:25). Caleb was in good company!

We too must take seriously our Lord's warnings of persecution. Persecution has continued throughout church history, and continues today. We may not face physical stoning today (though in some places Christians do), but verbal stones may well be thrown at us. Paul says, 'All who desire to live godly in Christ Jesus will suffer persecution' (2 Tim. 3:12).

However, what is particularly tragic about the threat against Caleb and Joshua (and in all these biblical examples) is that it was the Lord's people (at least nominally) who were talking of stoning them.

In the light of this, perhaps we need to pray for ourselves—not only that we would be able to endure persecution, but also that we might never become persecutors ourselves; that the stones will never be found in our hands.

The immoral majority

One obvious lesson from all this is that the majority are not always right.

In 1979, the American Baptist minister Jerry Falwell founded Moral Majority, claiming that this was the voice of the 'silent majority' of American people. One would like to believe so, but, sadly, the majority are not always on the side of the truth. There is sometimes an 'immoral majority' on the side of evil.

That clearly was the case here. It was the *majority* who spoke of stoning Caleb and Joshua—not just a handful of hotheads, not just a few extremists, but the vast majority of Israelites, including many of the tribal leaders.

This has its political implications. Many nations pride themselves on their democracy, and rightly so. As Winston Churchill famously said in 1947, 'It has been said that democracy is the worst form of Government—except for all those other forms that have been tried.' Democracy works, provided the people are well informed and rational, and are not pressurized in any way or swayed by unhelpful influences. Those perfect conditions are rarely achieved! The worst example of a democratic disaster was the election of Hitler, but there are no doubt many others.

In the Bible, the majority are often disastrously wrong. Think of the crowd in Jerusalem, crying out, 'Crucify Him!' (Mark 15:13); or the crowd in Ephesus, crying out, 'Great is Diana of the Ephesians!' (Acts 19:28); or the crowd in Jerusalem demanding Paul's death (Acts 22:22).

The Israelites at Kadesh are another tragic example: misinformed, irrational, swayed perhaps by crowd hysteria, they ended up rebelling against God and threatening to murder his servants. We could even think of it as a democratic disaster. The spies had 'voted' 10–2 against Caleb and Joshua's 'minority report' (enough to secure a verdict in a modern British court!), and the people had gone along with them, rather than listening to God or his servant, Moses.

The majority can sometimes be wrong even in the church. Churches are sometimes swept along by 'religious hysteria'. False doctrines and unbiblical rituals are accepted because they are widely held and practised. Sometimes sin is condoned because 'everyone does it', or because of 'changing opinions in the world'. Whatever we do must be tested by Scripture, and not simply by the number of people who agree with it. The Bible says, 'You shall not follow a crowd to do evil' (Exod. 23:2).

This is also true in church decision-making. Many different forms of church government exist, with varying degrees of power given to the congregation. Wherever we stand on this, we must always remember that human beings are fallible, and the majority are not always right.

But, equally, the majority are not always wrong! There can be a beautiful unity among God's people as the Spirit of God leads us into agreement. The apostles wrote after the Council of Jerusalem: 'It seemed good to the Holy Spirit, and to us ...' (Acts 15:28). That is surely how it should be.

The crowd at Kadesh Barnea, however, were not led by the Spirit: they were led by their own fear, and the result was disastrous.

The loneliness of faith

Another lesson is that we need to be prepared to stand alone.

Caleb, of course, was not quite alone. Joshua was with him, and so were Moses and Aaron. All the same, he must have felt very isolated, speaking up for God with the whole crowd 'breathing out threats and slaughter' against him.

There is a song that says, 'Dare to be a Daniel! Dare to stand alone.' We could equally say, 'Dare to be a Caleb!' Here is the whole song:

Standing by a purpose true,
Heeding God's command,
Honour them, the faithful few!
All hail to Daniel's band!

Dare to be a Daniel!
Dare to stand alone!
Dare to have a purpose firm!
Dare to make it known!

Mighty men are lost,
Daring not to stand,
Who for God had been a host,
By joining Daniel's band.

Many giants, great and tall,
Stalking through the land,
Headlong to the earth would fall,
If met by Daniel's band.

Hold the gospel banner high!
On to victory grand!
Satan and his hosts defy,
And shout for Daniel's band.[1]

'Daniel's band' has many famous members. David stood alone against Goliath. Elijah felt alone as he fled from Jezebel: 'I alone am left; and they seek to take my life' (1 Kings 19:10)—though there were actually seven thousand still faithful, of whom he was unaware. Jesus stood alone at his trial, all his disciples having forsaken him and fled. Paul says, 'At my first defense no one stood with me, but all forsook me. May it not be charged against them' (2 Tim. 4:16).

The great fourth-century theologian Athanasius stood 'alone' against the Arians in defence of the divinity of Christ. Some agreed with him, but many powerful voices were raised against him, including, at times, that of the emperor. People spoke of '*Athanasius contra mundum*' (Athanasius against the world).

Martin Luther stood 'alone' at the Diet of Worms, defending justification by faith. He had his supporters, including the Elector of Saxony, but all the great leaders of the Church of Rome were against him, and his life was in danger. But Luther stood firm: 'Here I stand; I can do no other.'

Caleb could have said the same.

We too may have to stand alone, or at least be part of a small minority.

Certainly in the world we are often in the minority. You may be the only Christian in your workplace, in your class at school or amongst your friends at university, or perhaps even in your own family. You may be a lone voice, speaking up for some moral cause, shouted down by everyone around you. You may even be a Christian in national or local government, very much aware of being in the minority. In our post-Christian, postmodern, post-truth society, we may find ourselves hopelessly out of line with the world around us, and we may have to face their contempt and hatred, and even legislation against us. Jesus warns us, 'If you were of the world, the world would love its own. Yet because you are not of the world, but I chose you out of the world, therefore the world hates you' (John 15:19).

Sadly, too, we may have to stand alone at times in the church. There are times when the church goes astray, drawn away by the world or confused by false doctrine. Then faithful Christians have a duty to stand firm. That can be hard, because we love our fellow Christians and have no desire to upset them. It would, however, be a failure of love to say nothing.

In the event, Caleb was unable to halt the tide of rebellion. The people of Israel had made their fatal decision and they must now bear the consequences. But Caleb had at least done what he could. And we must do the same. However hard it is, we must follow Caleb's example and stand firm for the truth. And this we can do because, like him, we are standing on the Rock.

And although people may reject us, and even threaten us, any rebellion against God is ultimately futile—as Israel was about to find out.

NOTES

1   Written by Philip Bliss in 1873 for the Sunday school at the First Congregational Church of Chicago. According to Ira D. Sankey in *My Life and the Story of the Gospel Hymns* (London: Hodder & Stoughton/Morgan & Scott, 1906), p. 82, it has the extraordinary distinction of having been banned by the Sultan of Turkey, along with another song by Bliss, 'Hold the Fort'!

Forty years in the wilderness (Num. 14:10–45)

There are some events that change the course of history. The gunshot that killed Archduke Franz Ferdinand in Sarajevo on 28 June 1914 sparked off a world war. Another gunshot in Dallas on 22 November 1963 left President Kennedy fatally wounded. There was a happier moment on 20 July 1969, when Neil Armstrong stepped onto the moon: 'One small step for [a] man; one giant leap for mankind.' And there was that terrible moment on 11 September 2001, when two planes crashed into the Twin Towers in New York.

The greatest of all world-changing events were Adam's sin in the Garden of Eden and Christ's death on the cross, bringing judgement and salvation to the world respectively. But the Bible records many other significant moments.

Israel's decision not to go into Canaan at Kadesh Barnea was one of them. The moment they said 'No', judgement came upon them. God condemned them to wander for forty years in the wilderness. God's plan had not changed; he had given the land to Israel, and he would not go back on that. But it would not happen now for another forty years.

Picture the scene. There they are on the borders of the land. The spies have given their report. Joshua and Caleb say 'Go'; the others say 'No'— and the people agree with them. There is a groundswell of rebellion, with talk of appointing new leaders and returning to Egypt. (Perhaps the ten spies, all tribal leaders, might fancy themselves for that task?) And there is talk of stoning Joshua and Caleb.

And then God appears in glory.

The glory of God

It must have been an awesome experience to see the glory of God.

It was not the first time they had seen it. The glory of God had 'appeared in the cloud' when God promised the manna (Exod. 16:10) and again when the Ten Commandments were given (Exod. 19:18; Deut. 5:24). The glory of the Lord 'rested on Mount Sinai' when Moses went up onto the mountain (Exod. 24:16). Moses saw the glory of the Lord from the cleft of the rock (Exod. 33:21–22), and his face shone afterwards. The tabernacle was filled with the glory of the Lord (Exod. 40:34). The glory of God appeared when the first sacrifices were offered (Lev. 9:23). Now, once again, 'the glory of the LORD appeared' in the tabernacle, at Kadesh Barnea, in the sight of all the people (Num. 14:10).

For Caleb and Joshua, that must have come as an enormous relief! God had stepped in to rescue them at the eleventh hour, as it were—rather like a policeman stopping a violent quarrel and saying, 'What's going on here?'

But for the Israelites, it was not a welcome sight. God knew what was going on. He knew their hearts; he knew the rebellious words they had been muttering—and he was angry. They deserved judgement, and he had come to judge them.

The glory of God appears also many times in the New Testament. The glory of the Lord shone around the shepherds at Bethlehem (Luke 2:9). John says, 'The Word became flesh and dwelt among us, and we beheld His glory' (John 1:14). Paul says that 'the God who commanded light to shine out of darkness … has shone in our hearts to give the light of the knowledge of the glory of God in the face of Jesus Christ' (2 Cor. 4:6).

When Christ returns, the whole world will see his glory: 'Then the sign of the Son of Man will appear in heaven, and then all the tribes of the earth will mourn, and they will see the Son of Man coming on the clouds of heaven with power and great glory' (Matt. 24:30). For Christians, that will be a welcome sight. He comes to rescue us out of all the troubles of this world, just as he rescued Caleb and Joshua. But for the lost, it will be a terrifying sight, as for them it means judgement—just as it did for the unbelieving Israelites at Kadesh Barnea.

God's judgement

God first spoke with Moses. 'How long will these people reject Me?' he asked; how long will they not believe in me, after all they have seen? He threatened to destroy them, which is what they deserved, and to start again with Moses (Num. 14:11–12).

God had spoken like this before. A similar threat and a similar offer were made after the golden calf incident (Exod. 32:7–10). Moses' answer now was the same as it was then: he ignored the personal offer and pleaded with the Lord to forgive his people.

First he reasoned with the Lord. 'The Egyptians will hear of it,' he said, 'and they'll tell the Canaanites. They've heard that you are among these people and that you lead them by a pillar of cloud and fire. If you kill them, they'll say you weren't able to bring them into the land' (see vv. 13–16).

Then he reminded God of his mercy, quoting the very words which God himself had spoken at Mount Sinai:

And now, I pray, let the power of my Lord be great, just as You have spoken, saying, 'The LORD is longsuffering and abundant in mercy, forgiving iniquity and transgression; but He by no means clears the guilty, visiting the iniquity of the fathers on the children to the third and fourth generation.' Pardon the iniquity of this people, I pray, according to the greatness of Your mercy, just as You have forgiven this people, from Egypt even until now. (vv. 17–19)

This is a superb example of intercessory prayer, and it points us to the greatest intercessor of all: our Lord Jesus Christ, who, of course, had a greater argument to set before his Father—his own death on the cross for our sins.

It is very telling that Moses speaks of the Lord *continually* forgiving his people 'from Egypt even until now', implying that they had continually sinned. If we are honest, we know that we have too. We could say, 'Forgive us our sins, as you have from our conversion, even until now.' And we have the wonderful promise that, 'if we confess our sins, He is faithful and just to forgive us our sins and to cleanse us from all unrighteousness' (1 John 1:9).

There is forgiveness for Israel as a *nation*, even here at Kadesh Barnea. The Lord said, 'I have pardoned, according to your word' (v. 20). That *generation*, however, would be judged. God begins by saying they will be excluded from the land:

But truly, as I live, all the earth shall be filled with the glory of the LORD—because all these men who have seen My glory and the signs which I did in Egypt and in the wilderness, and have put Me to the test now these ten times, and have not heeded My voice, they certainly shall not see the land of which I swore to their fathers. (vv. 21–23)

The charge is twofold: they had rebelled against God despite all they had seen, and they had rebelled repeatedly ('ten times' may just mean 'many times', though ten rebellions can actually be counted: Exod. 14:11; 15:24; 16:2, 20, 27; 17:2; 32:1; Num. 11:1, 4; 14:2). Enough is enough; they must now bear their punishment. Only one exception is made: 'But My servant Caleb, because he has a different spirit in him and has followed Me fully, I will bring into the land where he went, and his descendants shall inherit it' (v. 24; Joshua is added later).

The Lord now dismisses them: 'The Amalekites and the Canaanites dwell in the valley; tomorrow turn and move out into the wilderness' (v. 25). In other words, 'You were afraid of these people; go back, then, to the wilderness.'

He now spells out what will happen: 'The carcasses of you who have complained against Me shall fall in this wilderness, all of you who were numbered … from twenty years old and above. Except for Caleb the son of Jephunneh and Joshua the son of Nun, you shall by no means enter the land ...' (vv. 29–30).

Their children would enter in: 'Your little ones, whom you said would be victims, I will bring in, and they will know the land which you have despised' (v. 31). But even they would suffer: 'Your sons shall be shepherds in the wilderness ... and bear the brunt of your infidelity' (v. 33).

And it would last a full forty years: 'According to the number of the days in which you spied out the land, forty days, for each day you shall bear your guilt one year, namely forty years, and you shall know My rejection.' And he sets his seal on it: 'I the LORD have spoken this' (vv. 34–35).

Judgement, in fact, came immediately upon the ten spies: they 'died by the plague before the LORD' (v. 37); only Joshua and Caleb remained alive.

Israel now wept over their sin and wanted to go into the land, but it was too late. Moses warned them that God would not be with them, and he was right. They were defeated and driven back (v. 45). There was no escaping the judgement of God; their wilderness wanderings had begun.

There was mercy in all this. Most of them did not die immediately. They would see much of God's goodness, even in the wilderness. The nation itself did not perish, but remained God's people. And their children would enter into the land. Still, it was a heavy sentence.

Why was the Lord's judgement so severe in this case? After all, we have all given way to fear at times. Our hearts have failed us, and we have drawn back from doing what we knew the Lord wanted us to do—and yet judgement has not come down on us with this severity. We have all had rebellious thoughts at times. And yet, when we have come to our senses and returned to the Lord, we have found him ready and willing to forgive— just as the Bible says he will be. What was different about this case?

Partly, it was the importance of the occasion. The whole purpose of the exodus was to bring them into the Promised Land—and they had refused. The opportunity to go into the land was a golden opportunity which past generations would have loved to have—and they had spurned it.

There was also the inexcusable nature of their unbelief. They had seen some of the greatest miracles the world has ever seen, and yet they still did not believe. In this respect, they were like the scribes and the Pharisees, who refused to believe even though they saw the miracles of Jesus himself.

There was also the persistent provocation—they had rebelled repeatedly. 'How *long* will these people reject Me?' (v. 11).

We could almost see Kadesh as a 'final exam'. After two years of teaching in the wilderness, their faith had been tested—and they had failed.

We should be grateful that the Lord is so gentle with us. Yet even under the new covenant, God's people are sometimes chastised for their sins. Paul warns the Corinthians that because of a wrong attitude to communion, 'many are weak and sick among you, and many sleep' (1 Cor. 11:30). And maybe some of us have 'wandered in the wilderness' for a while, because of our unbelief. We need to come back to the faith of Caleb.

Remembered throughout history

What happened that day at Kadesh Barnea reverberates throughout Scripture, almost always with honourable mention of Caleb and Joshua.

When Moses took a second census, in the Plains of Moab a whole generation later, it was solemnly recorded that God's word had been fulfilled. God's warnings of judgement are no idle threat!

These are those who were numbered … six hundred and one thousand seven hundred and thirty … But among these there was not a man of those who were numbered … in the Wilderness of Sinai. For the Lord had said of them, 'They shall surely die in the wilderness.' So there was not left a man of them, except Caleb the son of Jephunneh and Joshua the son of Nun. (Num. 26:51, 64–65)

Again, when the Reubenites and Gadites asked to inherit land east of the Jordan, Moses reminded them of God's judgement at Kadesh Barnea: 'So the LORD's anger was aroused on that day, and He swore an oath, saying, "Surely none of the men who came up from Egypt, from twenty years old and above, shall see the land ... except Caleb the son of Jephunneh, the Kenizzite, and Joshua the son of Nun, for they have wholly followed the LORD' (Num. 32:10–12). Their request was allowed, but only if they helped their brethren conquer the land, rather than discouraging them as the ten spies did.

Moses mentioned it again in Deuteronomy 1 as part of his retrospect of the past forty years, as they stood again on the borders of the land, about to enter in, and he again mentioned Caleb and Joshua with honour:

And the LORD ... was angry, and took an oath, saying, 'Surely not one of these men of this evil generation shall see that good land of which I swore to give to your fathers, except Caleb the son of Jephunneh; he shall see it, and to him and his children I am giving the land on which he walked, because he wholly followed the LORD.' (Deut. 1:34–36)

He recalled how God was angry with him also for their sakes and excluded even him; as a result, Joshua would now lead them into the land instead (Num. 20:12 attributes this to the incident when Moses struck the rock in anger, but the problem went back to Kadesh).

He was speaking, of course, to the children of that 'evil generation', now grown up, who forty years previously had 'no knowledge of good or evil', with Joshua standing by, ready to take over. He was saying, in effect, 'Don't make that mistake again. Go in now and possess the land.'

Jesus referred to the unbelieving people of his own day as 'an evil generation' (Luke 11:29), echoing Deuteronomy 1.

Kadesh Barnea is remembered also in the Psalms, notably in Psalm 95, quoted and applied to us in Hebrews 3:

Chapter 6

Today, if you will hear His voice,
'Do not harden your hearts, as in the rebellion,
As in the day of trial in the wilderness,
When your fathers tested Me;
They tried Me, though they saw My work.
For forty years I was grieved with that generation,
And said, "It is a people who go astray in their hearts,
And they do not know My ways."
So I swore in My wrath,
"They shall not enter My rest"' (Ps. 95:7–11)

Psalm 106 also remembers it, and links it with the exile, recalling how God had

… raised His hand in an oath against them,
To overthrow them in the wilderness,
To overthrow their descendants among the nations,
And to scatter them in the lands. (vv. 26–27)

Paul also remembers it, drawing a comparison with Christian experience: 'Moreover, brethren, I do not want you to be unaware that all our fathers were under the cloud, all passed through the sea … But with most of them God was not well pleased, for their bodies were scattered in the wilderness … Now all these things happened to them as examples, and they were written for our admonition' (1 Cor. 10:1, 5, 11).

For the unbelieving Israelites, Kadesh Barnea was a disaster. It was the end of a dream, and the beginning of a nightmare. It was a forty-year sentence upon the whole nation, and a death sentence upon most of them. And they must live their lives now with the knowledge that God was not pleased with them.

With Caleb, however, God *was* pleased, and we must now consider why.

Commended by God (Num. 14:24; Josh. 14:9)

I t is always good to be praised. As a child, I actually looked forward to my school report, because it was usually good. I was devastated when, occasionally, there was a word of criticism. Years later, working in the City, we had an annual appraisal. I lived in hopes of my boss praising my performance and giving me a pay rise; it never happened!

The praise of our parents, our friends, our fellow Christians—it all matters to us. But what must it be to be praised by God? That was Caleb's happy experience. God said of him: 'But My servant Caleb, because he has a different spirit in him and has followed Me fully, I will bring into the land where he went, and his descendants shall inherit it' (Num. 14:24).

Caleb must have treasured those words. He recalled them forty-five years later, when they reached the land: 'Moses swore on that day, saying, "Surely the land where your foot has trodden shall be your inheritance and your children's forever, because you have wholly followed the LORD my God"' (Josh. 14:9).

What was it, precisely, that God praised in Caleb? Two words stand out: he was *different* and he had followed the Lord *fully*.

A man who was different

Caleb, in many respects, was the *same* as everyone else. Like Elijah and all the other heroes of the Bible, he was 'a man with a nature like ours' (James 5:17), with the same human weaknesses.

He was not immune to fear, like the German hero Siegfried, who had never known fear. Caleb was certainly not sinless. The Bible says 'all have sinned and fall short of the glory of God' (Rom. 3:23), and that includes

Caleb. He had gone through the same experiences as everyone else: 'all our fathers were under the cloud, all passed through the sea' (1 Cor. 10:1). He had seen the same miracles, heard the same promises, gone through the same trials.

Yet God says Caleb was different. How?

He was different, firstly, from the ten spies. All twelve of the spies were tribal leaders—'heads of the children of Israel' (Num. 13:3), well-respected men, trusted by Moses. They had all received, and obeyed, the same instructions. They had all gone through the same land and seen the same sights: the fruitful fields, the fortified cities, the giants towering over them. But whereas the ten spies were overcome with fear, Caleb (and Joshua) remembered God's promise. The ten spies saw the potential dangers; Caleb and Joshua saw the promised victory. Therefore they came back with a different report and different advice.

The difference was faith. Caleb believed the Lord; the others did not. In that respect, he was head and shoulders above the rest. He was the true giant!

He was different also from the people. They too were consumed by fear, but they were also rebellious in heart. They had been talking for months about going back to Egypt. With every slight problem that arose, they were full of doubts about this whole Promised Land Project. Could God bring them into the land of Canaan? Did he have any intention of doing so? Would he simply abandon them and leave them to be killed? They evidently thought that possible. They had been muttering against Moses ever since they left Egypt, no matter how many miracles he performed. They had 'an evil heart of unbelief' (Heb. 3:12); they had 'rejected' the Lord (Num. 14:11); they were an 'evil congregation' who complained against God (Num. 14:27). And they were full of hatred towards the servants of God, being ready to stone Joshua and Caleb, as they had thought of doing to Moses.

Caleb, in contrast, believed God's word, and nothing would cause him to question it. God had *given* them the land; that was enough for Caleb.

However many giants there might be—and he had seen them; the people hadn't—he was confident God would overcome them. God had shown his power in the past, over the Egyptians and the Amalekites; why should they doubt him now? Caleb had no doubts.

Caleb loved God's people, however sinful they were, however much they hated him. That was why he tried to persuade them. He might have been angry with them, as God was, but *he* was not taking up stones against *them*. But, above all, he loved God and wanted to see God glorified by victory, whereas the people only seemed to be concerned with their own safety.

The people resented this difference—so much so that they threatened to kill him.

The wicked have always hated the righteous. As John says: 'This is the message that you have heard from the beginning, that we should love one another, not as Cain, who was of the wicked one and murdered his brother. And why did he murder him? Because his works were evil and his brother's righteous' (1 John 3:11–12).

A godly man shows up the ungodly, and without even a word being said, the comparison condemns the ungodly. That is one reason why the people crucified Christ—because he was different, a godly man in an ungodly generation.

We too are called to be different. We are called to be 'the light of the world' in the midst of darkness, salt in the midst of corruption (Matt. 5:13–16). We are called to be holy in a world that loves sin and hates holiness. We are called to love God in a world that loves only itself. We are called to obey God in a world that resents any attempt to impose God's Law upon them. We are called to follow Christ in a world that pays lip service to him as a great teacher, but rejects his teaching. We are called to trust in Christ in a world that says, 'We can manage on our own.' We are called to be servants of the King in a world that says, 'We will not have this man to reign over us' (Luke 19:14).

Being different does not mean being eccentric (though people might think us odd). We are not called to be different just for the sake of being different—speaking differently, dressing differently (except insofar as we speak graciously and dress modestly). When I worked in London, I used to see members of the Hare Krishna sect go around the streets in their yellow robes, chanting. They were certainly different! But that is not what the Lord is looking for.

Caleb, we are told, had a different *spirit*. That is what God wants. Caleb was not marked out (as far as we know) by his dress or speech. What marked him out was his faith, which everyone noticed—for better or worse.

Being different will mark us out in the eyes of the world, and we may well face opposition, as Caleb did. But we must have the courage to stand out—to be the people who do not swear, who refuse to laugh at ungodly jokes, who love the weak and vulnerable even when everyone else rejects them, who forgive when everyone else is crying out for revenge; who love the Lord, his Word, his people and his Day, when all these things mean nothing to others, and sometimes even bring us into conflict with them.

One of the most extraordinary images in the Bible is in Jeremiah 12:9, where God's people are described as a 'speckled bird' (KJV) attacked by all the other birds. The context is judgement—Jerusalem abandoned to its enemies—but we can apply it to the church. We are sometimes attacked just because we are different. Caleb was a 'speckled bird' hated by all the 'birds' around him, who threatened to stone him because he was faithful and they were not. We must be prepared to be 'speckled birds'!

Any difference between us and the world is ultimately, however, the result of grace. Paul challenges the Corinthians, 'Who makes you differ from another? And what do you have that you did not receive?' (1 Cor. 4:7). In the context, he is speaking ironically. The Corinthians were boasting about their gifts and Paul wanted to stop that. But there is a broader principle here. If there is anything good in our lives, we have God to thank for it. It was God who had made Caleb what he was, and it is

God who makes us what we are, and to God must go the praise. He alone can give us the courage and conviction to be different.

A man who followed the Lord fully

The second reason why God praised Caleb was because he 'followed [the Lord] fully'. Indeed, that was the key difference between him and others.

Others, to be fair, followed the Lord partially. Even the ten spies were not totally unfaithful—far from it. They were recognized, remember, as leaders in Israel—they would not have achieved respect like that without showing some faith in the God of Israel. They were trusted by Moses, who would surely have looked for faithful men. They had faithfully obeyed the command they were given, to explore the land. They had not simply looked around a few villages and then gone back to write up their report. At great risk they had travelled from the far north to the far south, noting everything that seemed relevant. They clearly wanted to do a good job. But there it ended. Confronted by those giants, they no longer had the faith to say, 'Go in', though they knew God had given them the land. No doubt they could make excuses. They were simply being wise, being cautious, thinking of the best interests of the people, not wanting them to rush into war when they were not ready. But at the end of the day, they had fallen short of God's expectations. They had delivered a false report, twisted the facts, given the wrong advice and 'discouraged the heart' of their brethren (Num. 32:9).

Caleb, in contrast, had gone the whole way. He had faithfully explored the land, and faithfully delivered his report without any twisting of the facts, and he had faithfully encouraged the people to go in. And when the people rebelled, Caleb remained faithful, standing firm for the truth, at the risk of his own life.

The people themselves were not totally unfaithful. They had faithfully followed Moses out of Egypt, faithfully kept the Passover, and faithfully crossed the Red Sea. Hebrews counts the *people* as 'heroes of faith' at the

Red Sea: 'By faith they passed through the Red Sea as by dry land, whereas the Egyptians, attempting to do so, were drowned' (Heb. 11:29).

But somehow their faith had faltered; rather like those Egyptian chariot wheels which fell off in the Red Sea, the wheels had come off their faith, and by the time they got to Kadesh Barnea there was not a lot left of it. They had followed the Lord so far, but they were not willing to follow him any further. They refused to follow him into the land, and therefore they were condemned to the wilderness. They had *not* 'wholly followed' the Lord (Num. 32:11).

Caleb, in contrast, was willing to follow the Lord all the way—out of Egypt, through the Red Sea, through the wilderness, and, if it were possible, into Canaan, however many giants and fortified cities there might be. He was, after all, following the *Lord,* the Maker of heaven and earth, the King of all nations, the Commander of the army of the Lord, who could never be beaten. He would happily follow the Lord wherever he might lead him.

We could sum it all up by saying that Caleb was a man of faith, and a faithful man. There are not many like him. 'Most men will proclaim each his own goodness, but who can find a faithful man?' (Prov. 20:6).

Caleb is singled out among 603,550 men. Joshua, it is true, receives the same accolade—he also had 'wholly followed' the Lord (Num. 32:12). And it says of Moses that he was 'faithful in all [God's] house' (Heb. 3:5). But Caleb stands out as an exceptional man. And he is set before us as an example.

Wholeheartedness

God expects us all to be wholehearted like Caleb.

When asked, 'Which is the great commandment in the law?' Jesus replied, 'You shall love the LORD your God with all your heart, with all your soul, and with all your mind' (Matt. 22:36–37, quoting Deut. 6:5). And that love is expressed in obedience—ideally total obedience, keeping *all* God's commandments (Deut. 6:2). Joshua was commanded: 'Be strong and very courageous, that you may observe to do according to all the law which Moses My servant commanded you; do not turn from it to the right hand or to the left, that you may prosper wherever you go' (Josh. 1:7).

The Bible also speaks of wholehearted worship. David says, 'I will praise you, O LORD, with my whole heart' (Ps. 9:1). Psalm 119 repeatedly speaks of wholeheartedness:

Blessed are those who keep His testimonies,
Who seek Him with the whole heart! (v. 2)

With my whole heart I have sought You.
Oh, let me not wander from Your commandments! (v. 10)

Give me understanding, and I shall keep Your law;
Indeed, I shall observe it with my whole heart. (v. 34)

I entreated Your favor with my whole heart.
Be merciful to me according to Your word. (v. 58)

The proud have forged a lie against me,
But I will keep Your precepts with my whole heart. (v. 69)

I cry out with my whole heart;
Hear me, O LORD! (v. 145)

It is reassuring to notice there, in verse 58, that wholeheartedness is not inconsistent with needing God's mercy! We fall far short in our commitment, but God is gracious and ready to forgive.

Jeremiah speaks of wholehearted repentance: 'They shall be My people, and I will be their God; for they shall return to Me with their whole heart' (Jer. 24:7). Not half-heartedly but wholeheartedly!

Jesus expects wholehearted discipleship. When Jesus said to Peter and Andrew, 'Follow Me, and I will make you fishers of men', they had no doubt what it meant: 'They immediately left their nets and followed Him' (Matt. 4:19–20). No hesitation, no reservations, no holding back. From now on they would go wherever Jesus led them. Similarly with Matthew, the tax collector: when Jesus said, 'Follow Me', immediately 'he arose and followed Him' (Matt. 9:9).

Jesus warns us that the cost could be great: 'If anyone desires to come after Me, let him deny himself, and take up his cross, and follow Me' (Matt. 16:24). When he says, 'My sheep hear My voice … and they follow Me' (John 10:27), he is not thinking of a casual saunter into the next field. He expects them to follow him wherever he goes—in green pastures, by still waters, and through the 'valley of the shadow of death' (Ps. 23:4). He always leads us 'in the paths of righteousness'—but even that can be hard, requiring frequent self-denial. But he will be with us: that is our comfort and strength. He goes before us—but we must follow. True believers 'follow the Lamb wherever He goes' (Rev. 14:4).

Such wholehearted discipleship is only reasonable. God has been wholeheartedly faithful to us, and we must be wholeheartedly faithful to him. Jesus gave himself wholeheartedly for us; we must give ourselves wholeheartedly to him.

A lifelong commitment

God expects from us also a lifelong commitment.

For Caleb, 'following the Lord fully' meant not only being faithful at Kadesh Barnea—giving his report and standing firm when they threatened to stone him—but also following the Lord faithfully for forty years in the wilderness, and after that, in the Promised Land.

For most of the apostles, following the Lord fully would actually mean martyrdom. Jesus made that abundantly clear to Peter:

'When you were younger, you girded yourself and walked where you wished; but when you are old, you will stretch out your hands, and another will gird you and carry you where you do not wish.' This He spoke, signifying by what death he would glorify God. [Tradition has it that Peter was crucified.] And when He had spoken this, He said to him, 'Follow me.' (John 21:18–19)

We each have our own path to walk. When Peter asked about John, he was told not to worry about him; 'You follow Me' (John 21:22). Our path may be different from Caleb's, as Caleb's was different from Peter's. But wherever the Lord leads us, we must go. As the old hymn-writers put it:

True hearted, whole hearted, faithful and loyal,
King of our lives, by Thy grace we will be.[1]

What He says we will do,
Where He sends we will go;
Never fear, only trust and obey![2]

Caleb's reward

Such total commitment brings its rewards.

Perhaps the greatest reward for Caleb was simply to be praised by God. People might have hated him and talked of stoning him, but God had praised him, and the praise of God matters more than the praise of men.

It was said of some of the rulers in Jerusalem that 'they loved the praise of men more than the praise of God' (John 12:43). Not so with Caleb. Paul says, 'he is a [true] Jew who is one inwardly … whose praise is not from men but from God' (Rom. 2:29). Caleb qualified as a true Jew.

For the Christian, the ultimate reward is to hear the Lord say, 'Well done, good and faithful servant' (Matt. 25:21).

No doubt it was precious to Caleb also, however, to be vindicated publicly. Moses told the people what God had said (Num. 14:39), so everyone knew that God approved of Caleb.

But there was also a more tangible reward. God said, 'I will bring [Caleb] into the land where he went, and his descendants shall inherit it' (Num. 14:24).

Now, at first sight, this is nothing more than God had promised to all Israel: 'I will bring you into the land which I swore to give to Abraham, Isaac, and Jacob; and I will give it to you as a heritage' (Exod. 6:8). Nothing extra was added. Caleb was not given a double portion of land, or the very best of the land, as a special reward for being better than others. God simply confirmed his share in the covenant. He and his children would inherit the land.

But that in itself was precious. The Lord was effectively renewing his covenant with Caleb, just as he had done with Isaac and Jacob. Along with Joshua, Caleb could claim to be a new 'father of the faithful', like Abraham.

God was also reassuring him that he would not come under judgement like the rest of Israel. Unlike them, he would survive those forty years in the wilderness, and inherit the land.

This is similar to the promise made to the faithful in Sardis: 'He who overcomes shall be clothed in white garments, and I will not blot out his name from the Book of Life; but I will confess his name before My Father and before His angels' (Rev. 3:5). Indeed, all the promises to the 'overcomers' in Revelation 2 and 3—eating from the tree of life, not being hurt by the second death, the hidden manna, the white stone, and so on—are really just the basic blessings awaiting all true believers.

There are rewards in heaven. The Parable of the Talents speaks mysteriously of 'ruling over cities'. Whatever that means, it is sure to be good! But the greatest reward is simply to be told, 'Well done … Enter into the joy of your lord.'

For Caleb, simply entering Canaan was a wonderful reward. And to know that his descendants would inherit also was a bonus. Whether he had any children at this stage we are not told, but he certainly did later—a daughter, Achsah (Josh. 15:16), and three sons, Iru, Elah and Naam (1 Chr. 4:15). These children would, and did, inherit the land with him.

Furthermore, it was 'the land where he went'. That could, of course, mean anywhere in Canaan, but Caleb applied it especially to Hebron (Josh. 14:12), the very place where they had seen the giants, with the Valley of Eshcol nearby. That would indeed be a great prize, and Caleb no doubt looked forward to it.

If we are faithful, we too can look forward to the reward—not because we deserve it, but because, like Caleb, we serve a faithful God who has promised good things to his servants—and his word never fails.

Commended by God

Caleb, then, was commended by God. God was pleased with him.

He is not alone in this. It is said of Enoch that 'he had this testimony, that he pleased God' (Heb. 11:5). David is described as 'a man after [God's] own heart' (1 Sam. 13:14; Acts 13:22). God says of Job (to Satan!), 'Have you considered My servant Job, that there is none like him on the earth, a blameless and upright man, one who fears God and shuns evil?' (Job 1:8). The greatest example of all is Jesus himself. God says of him, 'Behold! My Servant whom I uphold, My Elect One in whom My soul delights!' (Isa. 42:1); and again, at his baptism, 'This is My beloved Son, in whom I am well pleased' (Matt. 3:17).

We too must make it our aim to be pleasing to God—like Caleb.

NOTES

1   Frances Ridley Havergal (1836–1879).
2   John Henry Sammis (1846–1919), 'When We Walk with the Lord'.

The wilderness years (Num. 15–Deut. 34)

Israel's journey through the wilderness is one of history's epic journeys: a whole nation travelling for forty years to its final home. It is often taken as an allegory of the Christian life, travelling through the wilderness of this world to the heavenly Canaan. This is the theme of William Williams' great hymn:

Guide me, O Thou great Jehovah,
Pilgrim through this barren land.
I am weak, but Thou art mighty;
Hold me with Thy powerful hand.

The hymn speaks of the bread of heaven, the crystal fountain and the cloudy pillar, and comes to a climax with the crossing of the Jordan:

When I tread the verge of Jordan,
Bid my anxious fears subside;
Death of deaths, and hell's destruction,
Land me safe on Canaan's side.

Bunyan's *Pilgrim's Progress* echoes the same theme. His allegory is more complex, involving all kinds of English landscapes—meadows, towns and castles, rather than a wilderness—but the grand climax is the crossing of the river to the Celestial City, just like the crossing of the Jordan.

The Bible itself compares the wilderness experience with the Christian life. Jesus, for example, speaks of himself as the Bread of Life, and Paul applies lessons from the wilderness to the church at Corinth.

It is an excellent allegory—though it does have its limitations. Israel's journey took forty years as a judgement from God, when it could have taken two. No one would suggest that a long life on earth is a punishment from God! The earthly Canaan also was rather different from the heavenly Canaan. There were wars to be fought there, and the people would later suffer conquest and exile. Our 'heavenly Canaan' is perfect, and it is ours for ever.

Israel's journey

Israel's 'forty years in the wilderness' appears to be the total time taken to travel from Egypt to the Jordan, the time from Egypt to Kadesh being 'taken into consideration' when God sentenced them to 'forty years' in Numbers 14.

Moses tells us the route they took in Numbers 33:1–49, counting forty encampments from Rameses in Egypt to the Plains of Moab. Unfortunately, most of these places are unknown to us, and we cannot easily trace the journey on a map. They left Sinai just over a year after leaving Egypt (Num. 10:11–12), and reached Kadesh soon afterwards (eleven days' march plus encampments, Deut. 1:2). They were in Kadesh 'many days' (Deut. 1:46). Then their wanderings began: 'We turned and journeyed into the wilderness of the Way of the Red Sea, as the LORD spoke to me, and we skirted Mount Seir for many days' (Deut. 2:1). What a sense of weariness we get from those words! Moses speaks of 'trudging through this great wilderness' (Deut. 2:7).

What a moment it must have been for Caleb when they 'turned' and went off into the wilderness. What did he think? Was he angry, tearful, or just resolutely confident in the promises of God? Did he look back wistfully towards Canaan, or did he march forwards into the wilderness, quietly submissive to the will of God? We are not told, but it must have been an emotional moment.

It was an emotional moment too for Israel, marching into the unknown, with the judgement of God upon them. Yet the Lord had not deserted them. They were still his people; he was still with them, protecting and providing. Moses says: 'These forty years the LORD your God has been with you; you have lacked nothing' (Deut. 2:7b). They were still heading as a nation for the Promised Land. A whole generation would die (except Caleb and Joshua), but their children would inherit the land.

God's long-term plan was still the same! Thirty-eight years after leaving Kadesh, when all the 'guilty generation' had died, they crossed over the Valley of the Zered (Deut. 2:14), came into Moab and reached the River Jordan. God had brought them safely to their promised destination.

He will do the same for us. Despite all our sins, he will bring us to heaven. Jesus said (in the context of the wilderness imagery of John 6, where he calls himself the Bread of Life, the true manna sent down from heaven): 'This is the will of the Father who sent Me, that of all He has given Me I should lose nothing, but should raise it up at the last day' (John 6:39).

Caleb in the wilderness

Where was Caleb all these years? Obviously, he was travelling with the Israelites, sharing in all the weariness of the journey. When a nation is under judgement, even good people sometimes have to share the suffering with them.

Nothing is said, however, of Caleb personally throughout these years. He has become, as far as the narrative is concerned, the invisible man!

We can work out a few details. We know he was forty at Kadesh (Josh. 14:7). He would have been fifty, sixty, seventy in the wilderness—though still fit and well (Josh. 14:11). We also know he had a family—a wife (presumably), three sons, Iru, Elah and Naam (1 Chr. 4:15), and a daughter, Achsah (Judg. 1:13), though we are not told when they were born. By the age of forty, most men would have been married, so he may have had the children before they reached Kadesh; maybe even in Egypt.

Certainly, they were with him in the wilderness. We also know he had a younger brother, Kenaz, and a nephew, Othniel, who later married Achsah (Judg. 1:13). Kenaz presumably died in the wilderness.

We have no means of telling what his thoughts were in those wilderness years. We are not told, and it would be presumptuous to guess. We can, however, imagine what *our* thoughts might have been!

To begin with, it would take superhuman grace not to feel some measure of resentment that Israel had rejected our advice. 'If only they had listened,' we might say, 'we could all have been in the land by now, rather than wandering in this desert!'

It would be easy to look with contempt on these Israelites, who had been too scared to go in and conquer the land. We might have felt some 'righteous anger' at the way they had rebelled against the Lord, and some unrighteous bitterness that we and our children were having to suffer for it.

Also, it would not be easy to live for thirty-eight years with people who had threatened to kill us. Victims of violence today are sometimes protected by the courts from contact with their aggressors. A restraining order might be placed upon them, ordering them not to come, perhaps, within a mile of their victim. But there was no restraining order protecting Caleb and his family! Every day they would see people who might, if they had been given a few more minutes, have murdered him. It is hard to trust someone who has threatened to kill you!

It might have been awkward also, being one of the leaders of Israel, when the other leaders had made the wrong choice at Kadesh.

There would also be the heartache of seeing friends and family die in the wilderness. It is not unusual for older people to have the sadness of losing friends. It is often said that when you are in your twenties, you are always attending weddings, but when you are in your sixties, it is all funerals. But Caleb's friends were dying while he was still in his forties. By the end, a whole generation gap had opened up between him and the rest of Israel.

Whether Caleb struggled with any of these thoughts we are not told, but it would be amazing if he did not.

What we do know is that Caleb travelled faithfully with his fellow Israelites, enduring all that they endured.

So far as we know, he never thought of leaving them. How could he? God was with them, and if he went off on his own, he would be going without God. There was no suggestion of gathering some supporters and forming a new nation, or of taking a few warriors and going off to conquer Canaan for himself. God's promise to Caleb was a promise for the future. If he had tried to conquer Hebron straightaway, he would have had no more success than the Israelites did when they tried to go into Canaan as an afterthought (Num. 14:39–45). With God, all things are possible; without God, nothing is possible.

So far as we know, he never caused Moses any problems. He never attempted to set himself up as a rival leader. He did not support the rebellion of Korah. He was content to serve God under Moses and Joshua.

Caleb loved God's people and was loyal to them; he even later referred to the ten spies as his 'brethren' (Josh. 14:8).

In this commitment to Israel, he was like his leader, Moses, who, even in Egypt, chose 'rather to suffer affliction with the people of God than to enjoy the passing pleasures of sin' (Heb. 11:25) and later declined the opportunity to go off on his own, even though God had *invited* him to do so.

He was also like our Lord, who gave up the riches of heaven and came down into a world of suffering, living among us, travelling with us, as it were, through the wilderness of this world. That is the implication of John 1:14: 'The Word became flesh and dwelt [literally, 'tabernacled'] among us'—though Christ went further, not only living among us, but also dying for us on the cross; not merely suffering *with* us, like Moses or Caleb, but suffering *for* us.

What sustained Caleb through those wilderness years?

Caleb's own character helped, no doubt. But more important were the promises of God—both national and personal. The present might be hard, but the future was glorious, and the future was sure, because God had spoken.

In the words of the old hymn, Caleb was 'standing on the promises of God':

Standing on the promises of Christ my King,
Through eternal ages let His praises ring;
Glory in the highest, I will shout and sing,
Standing on the promises of God.

Standing, standing,
Standing on the promises of God my Saviour;
Standing, standing,
I'm standing on the promises of God.

Standing on the promises that cannot fail,
When the howling storms of doubt and fear assail,
By the living Word of God I shall prevail,
Standing on the promises of God.[1]

We too need to stand on God's promises amidst all our trials. We have 'exceedingly great and precious promises' (2 Peter 1:4), both for the present and for the future. God has spoken, and we must trust in his Word.

Commitment to the church

From Caleb, we also need to learn commitment to the church in our 'wilderness journey'. How the church today needs faithful, loyal members who will travel supportively and uncomplainingly with their brothers and sisters! Sadly, Christians today are all too ready to separate or to stir up trouble at the least provocation.

There are, of course, occasions when it is right to separate. When a church has completely departed from the faith, it may be necessary to leave. The Reformers were right to leave the Church of Rome in the sixteenth century, but many church splits have occurred since then that are less easy to justify.

Had Israel stubbornly insisted on returning to Egypt, Caleb, Joshua and Moses would have been justified in marching on towards Canaan without them. Arguably, it would have been the Israelites who had separated from them, by departing from God! When a church goes completely the wrong way and cannot be persuaded to see sense, we may, sadly, have to continue alone.

There can also be legitimate personal reasons for moving from one church to another, but this should never be done lightly.

We should certainly never be a cause of division ourselves. It is always a tragedy when churches divide, and we should always endeavour to 'keep the unity of the Spirit in the bond of peace' (Eph. 4:3).

There are times when it is right to criticize the church, provided it is done gently, humbly and constructively. But it is all too easy to become negative, stirring up discontent. Caleb never fell into that trap.

We must always remember that it is God's church—just as Israel were God's people—and treat it with honour, thinking well of our fellow believers and supporting them, rather than undermining them.

It is really quite remarkable that Israel remained united throughout those forty years in the wilderness. From a human standpoint, we can attribute that largely to Moses' leadership. The gracious spirit of Caleb and Joshua must also have helped—though ultimately it was God who had kept them together. We must pray for unity in our churches today.

All the way my Saviour leads me

Little is said about those forty years in the wilderness, except at the beginning and the end. A kindly veil of silence is drawn over the years in between. Moses sums up the 'goodness and severity' of God in those years:

You shall remember that the LORD your God led you all the way these forty years in the wilderness, to humble you and test you, to know what was in your heart, whether you would keep His commandments or not. So He humbled you, allowed you to hunger, and fed you with manna which you did not know nor did your fathers know, that He might make you know that man shall not live by bread alone; but man lives by every word that proceeds from the mouth of God. Your garments did not wear out on you, nor did your foot swell these forty years. You should know in your heart that as a man chastens his son, so the LORD your God chastens you. (Deut. 8:2–5)

We may just notice the major events which Caleb would have witnessed.

Early on, there was the rebellion of Korah, described in Numbers 16. God dealt with this decisively: the earth opened up and the ringleaders were swallowed alive, and when others complained, a plague broke out. Aaron's rod then blossomed overnight, to prove his authority; it was never questioned again!

After thirty-eight years, in Numbers 20, they came to Kadesh[2] in the Wilderness of Zin, where Miriam died, and the people again complained of thirst. Moses again brought water out of the rock, but because he struck the rock in anger, rather than speaking to it as commanded, God was angry with him, and Moses was excluded from the land, only being allowed to see it from afar. Israel's way was then barred by the Edomites; Aaron died on Mount Hor; and there was conflict with the king of Arad.

Then there were more complaints: 'The people spoke against God and against Moses: "Why have you brought us up out of Egypt to die in this wilderness? For there is no food and no water, and our soul loathes this worthless bread [the manna!]' (Num. 21:5). We can only groan: will they never learn? Judgement came in the form of fiery serpents that bit the people, and many died.

But God was gracious. The people repented, and God commanded Moses to make the famous bronze serpent; whoever looked at it would live—a wonderful picture of Christ crucified, as Jesus says: 'As Moses lifted up the serpent in the wilderness, even so must the Son of Man be lifted up, that whoever believes in Him should not perish but have eternal life' (John 3:14–15).

The mood brightened as they crossed over into Moab in the fortieth year. They knew that their journey was coming to an end. A well was dug and the people sang,

Spring up, O well!
All of you sing to it—
The well the leaders sank,
Dug by the nation's nobles,
By the lawgiver, with their staves. (Num. 21:17–18)

Did Caleb, as one of the leaders, help dig this well, and sing this song?

Sihon, king of the Amorites, and Og, king of Bashan, were defeated—famous victories celebrated years later in the Psalms (Num. 21; Ps. 136:17–22).

Danger still lurked. Balak, king of Moab, hired Balaam to prophesy against them. God rebuked Balaam by the mouth of an ass (Num. 22) and instead Balaam prophesied glory for Israel. Even so, the Israelites were led astray by the women of Moab and committed idolatry; 24,000 died in a plague (Num. 25).

A second census was taken, of the new generation, the old having now passed away; more laws were promulgated; the Midianites were defeated; and the Reubenites, Gadites and the half-tribe of Manasseh settled east of the Jordan.

And so they came to the Plains of Moab, where Moses reminded them of all that had happened and of the laws God had given them, in the Book of Deuteronomy (which means 'Second Law'). Moses dramatically divided the people between two mountains, six tribes (including Caleb's tribe of Judah) standing on Mount Gerizim to bless the people, the other six on Mount Ebal to remind them of the curses of the law. The covenant was renewed, and Moses urged them to keep it: 'I call heaven and earth as witnesses today against you, that I have set before you life and death, blessing and cursing; therefore choose life' (Deut. 30:19). Joshua was appointed as the new leader of Israel (Deut. 31), the Law was written in a book, and Moses taught them a song and blessed them, before going up onto Mount Nebo to die, at the age of 120 (Deut. 34).

The scene was now set for the conquest of Canaan.

Caleb had lived through all these dramatic years; he had witnessed all these dramatic events, and heard first-hand all these dramatic words. This was now the moment he had been waiting for—the fulfilment of God's promises. He could look back with gratitude, and look forward with anticipation.

He could have sung Frances Jane van Alstyne's beautiful hymn:

All the way my Saviour leads me;
What have I to ask beside?
Can I doubt His tender mercy,
Who through life has been my guide?

We can sing this too. Whatever stage of the journey we have reached, it is God who has led us, and is leading us, and will lead us to the end.

NOTES

1   Russell Kelso Carter, 1886.
2   Some think this is the same as Kadesh Barnea; others, including Matthew Henry, think it is a different place.

Still strong at eighty-five (Josh. 1–14)

I t is a favourite device of film-makers to 'fast-forward' many years to show what happened later. The Bible does that with Caleb.

Caleb was introduced to us at the age of forty, as the faithful spy, boldly urging the Israelites to conquer Canaan, and receiving a promise that he would enter the land, even if they did not. Since then, he has not been mentioned. If nothing more had been said, we might have wondered, 'Whatever happened to Caleb? Did God keep his promise?' Joshua 14 gives us the answer: fast-forward, and there is Caleb, aged eighty-five, still strong and full of faith—and there is God fulfilling his word. There is a certain symmetry about it: Numbers 14 records the promise; Joshua 14 records the fulfilment.

Before we come to this, however, we need to look back over the early chapters of Joshua and the conquest of Canaan.

Seven years of war

When the First World War broke out in August 1914, there was widespread optimism that it would be 'all over by Christmas'. It was not!

Something similar might have been said of the conquest of Canaan. When it began, the Israelites might have expected a quick victory. They had a great leader, great promises, and great miracles to encourage them. The Jordan parted; the walls of Jericho came tumbling down. This would be easy!

But then the setbacks began, and it actually took seven years; and even then, there remained 'much land yet to be possessed' (Josh. 13:1).

Let us trace what happened.

The opening chapter of Joshua is one of the most encouraging in the Bible, as Joshua is given his 'marching orders':

Arise, go over this Jordan, you and all this people, to the land which I am giving to them … No man shall be able to stand before you all the days of your life; as I was with Moses, so I will be with you. I will not leave you nor forsake you. Be strong and of good courage, for to this people you shall divide as an inheritance the land … do not be afraid, nor be dismayed, for the LORD your God is with you wherever you go. (Josh. 1:2, 5–6, 9)

God had given them the land; to obtain it, though, they needed to conquer it. This might raise a few eyebrows today, especially as they were to leave 'nothing that breathes' alive (Deut. 20:16). God's promise to Israel coincided with God's judgement on the nations. It was a one-off command, and cannot be used to justify aggressive conquest today.

But it was God's command then. Spies were therefore sent to 'view the land, especially Jericho' (Josh. 2:1)—just as Caleb and Joshua had done half a lifetime before. They reported back that the city was afraid and ready to be taken (having promised to spare Rahab for protecting them—so 'nothing that breathes' is not quite to be taken literally: there could be exceptions!).

They now crossed the Jordan—miraculously, the waters parted for them, just as they had done at the Red Sea. The men were circumcised at Gilgal—this having been neglected in the wilderness—and a great Passover was kept.

Joshua then had a mysterious encounter. The 'Commander of the army of the LORD' (Josh. 5:14) said they were to march around Jericho, blowing trumpets, and the walls would fall. And that was what happened. 'Joshua fit the battle o' Jericho, an' the walls came tumbling down', so the old song has it—only he did not have to fight. As at the Red Sea, they only had to 'Stand still, and see the salvation of the LORD' (Exod. 14:13).

They could simply watch the walls collapse, and march straight in. God was in control, and God would give them the victory.

But then it all went 'pear-shaped'. The Israelites were actually defeated at Ai because of Achan's sin in keeping treasure for himself, and Joshua was deceived into making peace with the Gibeonites.

A great battle took place at Gibeon, when the sun stood still (Josh. 10), and Joshua went on to conquer the whole land. But it was not easy: 'Joshua made war a long time with all those kings. There was not a city that made peace with the children of Israel, except the Hivites, the inhabitants of Gibeon. All the others they took in battle' (11:18).

We often think of Canaan as a picture of heaven—our 'land of milk and honey'. But the conquest of Canaan could equally be taken as a picture of the Christian life—a long, hard struggle, with many ups and downs, in which we are 'more than conquerors through Him who loved us' (Rom. 8:37).

Caleb's testimony

Caleb, no doubt, had fought in all these wars. He was now an old man—indeed, the oldest man in Israel apart from Joshua: twenty years older than anyone else, the older generation having died in the wilderness. He (and Joshua) must surely have been regarded with awe by the younger generation. But for Caleb, 'the best was yet to come'.

With most of the land conquered, Joshua began distributing the land by lot (Josh. 14:2). He began with the tribe of Judah.

But first, Caleb stepped forward with a special request. He began by reminding Joshua of God's promise, forty-five years previously:

And Caleb the son of Jephunneh … said to him: 'You know the word which the LORD said to Moses the man of God concerning you and me in Kadesh Barnea. I was forty years old when Moses the servant of the LORD sent me from Kadesh Barnea to spy out the land, and I brought back word to him as it was in my heart. Nevertheless my brethren who went up with me made the heart of the people melt, but I wholly followed the LORD my God. So Moses swore on that day, saying, "Surely the land where your foot has trodden shall be your inheritance and your children's forever, because you have wholly followed the LORD my God."' (14:6–9)

He then gave this remarkable testimony to God's faithfulness:

And now, behold, the LORD has kept me alive, as He said, these forty-five years, ever since the LORD spoke this word to Moses while Israel wandered in the wilderness; and now, here I am this day, eighty-five years old. As yet I am as strong this day as on the day that Moses sent me; just as my strength was then, so now is my strength for war, both for going out and for coming in. (vv. 10–11)

And then he 'called in' that promise: 'Give me this mountain' (v. 12).

We will look at that later; but first, consider Caleb's testimony.

Kept alive

Caleb says first that God had 'kept [him] alive'. That in itself was remarkable. Caleb had endured all the hardships of the wilderness—hunger, thirst and weariness, marching with men much younger than himself, living in tents year after year, summer and winter. He had survived wars and plagues in the wilderness, and seven years of war in Canaan. God had been faithful. He had made him a promise, and Caleb could not die until it was fulfilled.

Every Christian can say, 'God has kept me alive'—and he has done so for a purpose. We have survived all kinds of dangers, including some that perhaps we were not even aware of. 'The angel of the LORD encamps all around those who fear Him, and delivers them' (Ps. 34:7). Praise God for that!

Chapter 9

Physically strong

Caleb, however, was more than alive—he was 'fighting fit', quite literally, as strong at eighty-five as he was at forty: 'just as my strength was then, so now is my strength for war' (14:11). This too was the gift of God.

He was not unique in this. Moses only began his life's work of leading Israel out of Egypt at the age of eighty, and when he died, at 120, 'his eyes were not dim nor his natural vigor diminished' (Deut. 34:7). He was, however, weary during the battle with Amalek, and needed elders because he was exhausted. The strongest of men may need help as old age takes its toll.

Moses himself was quite realistic about the effects of old age:

The days of our lives are seventy years;

And if by reason of strength they are eighty years,

Yet their boast is only labor and sorrow;

For it is soon cut off, and we fly away. (Ps. 90:10, 'A Psalm of Moses', written, some believe, in the wilderness as he saw a whole generation dying before him.)

Before the Flood, people lived to extraordinary ages (Methuselah being the oldest at 969); after the Flood, life expectancy fell rapidly. Abraham lived to 175, Isaac, 180—though long before that, 'his eyes were so dim that he could not see' (Gen. 27:1). Jacob lived to 147, but was regarded as an old man when he appeared before Pharaoh at 130 (Gen. 47:9). Joseph lived 'only' 110 years. Joshua also lived to 110 (Josh. 24:29), though before that he is called 'old, advanced in years' (Josh. 13:1). Gradually, the ages were falling to seventy years.

David lived to precisely seventy years (2 Sam. 5:4), but in his final days he was a shadow of his former self, struggling to keep warm (1 Kings 1:1). Yet this is called 'a good old age' (1 Chr. 29:28). Later kings had even shorter lives. Uzziah, for example, whose reign was the longest in the history of Judah, lived to only sixty-eight (2 Chr. 26:3), his son, Jotham, to only forty-one (2 Chr. 27:1).

Caleb, therefore, was doing very well to be fit and strong at eighty-five.

There have been remarkable men in our own times who have achieved great things in old age. Sir Winston Churchill was sixty-five when he became Britain's wartime Prime Minister, seventy-five when he became Prime Minister again in 1951. Ronald Reagan was still President of the United States at seventy-seven; his successor, George H. W. Bush, celebrated his ninetieth birthday with a parachute jump! No doubt readers will know of less famous men—perhaps relatives—who have astonished everyone with what they have done in old age.

But Caleb stands as a supreme example. Just a few years before this, Moses had given his blessing to the twelve tribes of Israel. To Asher he said: 'As your days, so shall your strength be' (Deut. 33:25). Caleb was of the tribe of Judah, not Asher, but in him these words were wonderfully fulfilled.

Spiritually strong

It was not just physical strength, however; it was also spiritual strength.

Caleb, of course, does not say this: he would have been far too humble! But his spirituality shines through in this chapter. His faith in God was undiminished. He remembered that promise from forty-five years before, and still expected it to be fulfilled. His heart was full of thanksgiving to God. He was still ready to fight for God. And he still believed that great things were possible if God was with him. He was an example to all Israel—and to us—of expecting great things from God and attempting great things for God, even at the age of eighty-five.

There are other biblical examples of spiritual strength in elderly people.

Barzillai was 'a very aged man, eighty years old', yet he 'provided supplies' to David when he was fleeing from Absalom (2 Sam. 19:31–39).

When offered a reward he said he could no longer enjoy food, drink and music, and did not expect to live long; so he asked instead for favour for his son, Chimham. He was limited in what he could do; unlike Caleb, he was not able to go out to war. But he did what he could, and was simply glad to be serving the king.

Anna (who incidentally was of the tribe of Asher) was 'a widow of about eighty-four years', yet she was still serving the Lord as a prophetess, fasting and praying night and day in the temple. And after she saw the infant Jesus, she 'spoke of Him to all those who looked for redemption in Jerusalem' (Luke 2:36–38). No one is too old for evangelism!

Jesus told Peter he would suffer martyrdom as an old man (John 21:18–19), implying that he would still remain faithful in old age, 'faithful unto death'. As a young man he had boasted that he would die for his Lord, but then he denied him (John 13:37–38). As an old man, he really would die for him. His spiritual strength increased with age!

Paul calls himself 'the aged' while in prison in Rome (Philem. 9). He evidently continued preaching for some while after that, before being re-arrested. Tradition has it that he too was martyred, having served God to the end.

John must have been very old when he was exiled to Patmos, if the common view is right that it was during the reign of Domitian. There is a tradition (going back to Jerome) that in extreme old age, having returned to Ephesus, John was carried into church and would simply say, 'Love one another.' Only a few words, yet what an impact they must have had! Even the most elderly can still say a few words of encouragement to others.

In church history, Polycarp stands out. Invited to renounce Christ and sacrifice to the Roman gods to save his life in the arena, he cried out: 'For eighty-six years I have been his servant, and he has never done me wrong. How can I blaspheme my King who saved me?'[1]

There is also John Wesley, still travelling around the country preaching, well into his eighties. He wrote in his journal on 1 January 1790, aged eighty-six: 'I am now an old man, decayed from head to foot. My eyes are dim; my right hand shakes much; my mouth is hot and dry every morning; I have a lingering fever almost every day; my motion is weak and slow. However, blessed be God, I do not slack my labour: I can preach and write still.'[2] He preached in my own city of Lincoln in July 1790, remarking that there was 'not so much fire' in the believers there, compared with those in York (though he commends their gentleness).[3] There was still plenty of fire in Wesley!

There are many examples in our own times of faithful Christians serving God at an advanced age. Dr Martyn Lloyd-Jones, for example, continued preaching long after he retired as minister at Westminster Chapel, his last sermon being given at the age of eighty. You can no doubt think of many other examples, perhaps in your own church.

Ageing well

The passing of the years has different effects on Christians.

Some mature with age, 'growing in grace and in the knowledge of our Lord Jesus Christ'. It is a joy to meet such saints, and we can all learn from them. They are still keen to serve the Lord; they may be unable to do what they used to do, but they are happy to do whatever they can. Youthful sins have been subdued, youthful errors have been sorted out, and although they will freely admit that they are far from perfect (age brings with it an increased awareness of sin, along with new temptations to add to the old ones), others can see in them the light of Christ, as they are more and more conformed to his image. With such people, 'the path of the just is like the shining light, that shines ever brighter unto the perfect day' (Prov. 4:18).

Others, sadly, 'go to seed' in old age. Perhaps they become irritable and crotchety (even more than the pains of old age can excuse). Perhaps over the years their faith has faded away, or they have become disillusioned. Perhaps they have embraced false doctrines, or compromised so much with the world that you can hardly tell they are Christians. Perhaps they have become bitter, refusing to forgive the hurts of the past. Perhaps they feel they have done enough, and just want to rest and do nothing. Perhaps they resent younger people for taking over from them, and complain about every change.

Maybe some older reader is reflecting ruefully that this last paragraph describes him or her better than the previous one! I sympathize. Having reached retirement myself, I know that I am not altogether free from some of these faults! We find out in old age what human nature is really like! Yet even in old age, we can still change; the Lord can still make us what we ought to be.

Caleb, however, had 'aged well' spiritually. In him Psalm 92 was fulfilled:

Those who are planted in the house of the LORD
Shall flourish in the courts of our God.
They shall still bear fruit in old age;
They shall be fresh and flourishing,
To declare that the LORD is upright;
He is my rock and there is no unrighteousness in Him. (Ps. 92:13–15)

The key to 'ageing well' lies in our relationship with the Lord. Those who 'bear fruit in old age' are those who are 'planted in the house of the LORD', trusting in the Lord, serving the Lord and drawing strength from the Lord; they are those who can say, 'The Lord is my rock.' Caleb could certainly have said that the Lord was his rock; that was the secret of his strength.

The danger of ageism
We live in an age that glorifies youth; old people are often seen as a

problem. How will we pay their pensions? How will we look after them? Life expectancy is increasing: in the UK, it is now eighty-one, with seventy-one years of healthy living. There are over 10 million people in the UK who are over sixty-five years old—16 per cent of the population. This is often seen as a burden; but it should be seen as a blessing. Older people can contribute so much to society! And when they do require care, we should treat them with respect: 'Honor your father and your mother,' the Bible says, a command which it links with our own longevity (Exod. 20:12)!

Churches also need to take the elderly seriously. Many churches focus, understandably, on the young, and youth work is undoubtedly very important. Yet old people can also be saved, old people are also part of the congregation, old people also have pastoral needs, and old people can also serve God. Never underestimate the elderly!

Caleb is a wonderful example. He seems to be saying to us, across the centuries, 'I may be eighty-five, but I am not finished yet!'

Of course, people age differently. Some really are exhausted by the time they are sixty. We should never use Caleb as a stick with which to beat old people: 'If Caleb could do it, you can!' The Bible honestly admits that old age can be hard. Solomon says,

Remember now your Creator in the days of your youth,
Before the difficult days come,
And the years draw near when you say, 'I have no pleasure in them.' (Eccles. 12:1)

He gives a beautiful, but sad, poetic picture of the reality of old age, with all its ailments and anxieties. Coping with old age is a challenge in itself, for which few are prepared.

We ought not to imagine, either, that we can suddenly, overnight, become like Caleb spiritually. Caleb's faith at eighty-five was the fruit of a whole life of faith.

Caleb was exceptional. Few of us will have his physical strength, and not all of us will attain to his spiritual strength. But Caleb shows what is possible. Many elderly people can still achieve great things—perhaps more than the church imagines; perhaps more than they imagine themselves.

Remember that when Moses counted the people, he was told to include 'every male ... from twenty years old and above—all who are able to go to war' (Num. 1:2–3). There was no upper age limit! We have in our midst today a vast army of elderly warriors, men and women, who can still 'fight' in old age. Let us not neglect them or write them off.

Imagine if Israel had written off Caleb as an old man, still 'going on' about what had happened forty-five years previously! Imagine if they had pensioned off Joshua and Caleb and tried to conquer Canaan without them. They might have been successful—but how much harder it would have been!

May there be many Calebs in our churches, still strong, physically and spiritually, at eighty-five—and may all our elderly brothers and sisters, whether strong or weak, know that they are still loved by God, and useful to him, and loved and appreciated by their younger brethren.

NOTES

1   Cited in Dr Richard Alderson, *The Early Christians: A Taster* (Bromley: Day One, 1997), p. 29.

2   *Wesley His Own Biographer: Selections from the Journals of the Rev. John Wesley, A. M., With the Original Account of His Death*, 1 January 1790 (London: Charles H. Kelly, 1891), p. 619.

3   Ibid., 1 July 1790, p. 623.

Give me this mountain (Josh. 14:12–15; 15:13–14)

Many great people are remembered for some striking quotation. Julius Caesar, for example, is remembered for his verdict on Britain: 'Veni, vidi, vici'—I came, I saw, I conquered. Queen Elizabeth I is famous for her speech at Tilbury: 'I have the body but of a weak and feeble woman, but I have the heart and stomach of a king, and a king of England too!' Winston Churchill is famous for many speeches, amongst them, 'We shall fight them on the beaches ...'

Caleb is famous—at least among Christians—for his request to Joshua: 'Give me this mountain!'

We could even call it a demand, since it was based not on Joshua's generosity, but on the promise of God, with which Joshua would not dare to argue; it is one of the most audacious demands in the Bible—a demand made, remember, when Caleb was eighty-five.

Caleb's demand

This remarkable request (or demand) is found in Joshua 14:12. Having reminded Joshua of God's promise, forty-five years previously, and having testified to God's faithfulness and the strength God had given him, he says: 'Now therefore, give me this mountain of which the LORD spoke in that day; for you heard in that day how the Anakim were there, and that the cities were great and fortified. It may be that the LORD will be with me, and I shall be able to drive them out as the LORD said.'

The mountain in question was the area around Hebron which Caleb had seen as a spy. The Anakim were the 'giants' who had so frightened the other spies that they had told the Israelites they were unable to conquer the land. They were still there. Presumably by now they were old men, like Caleb, but they were still 'giants' and it was still a formidable challenge he was taking on.

Forty-five years before, however, he had believed that with God's help they could defeat them; he believed that still, and he intended to prove his point—to drive out those giants and claim that mountain as his inheritance.

Caleb's patience

It is rather striking that Caleb had waited until now to make this request. It must have been on his heart for the previous forty-five years. It would have been quite understandable if, the moment they crossed the Jordan, Caleb had headed south to Hebron. But no, he had spent the last seven years fighting for Israel, conquering the land before claiming his inheritance. This shows Caleb's priorities—nation before self. It also shows extraordinary patience.

The Bible speaks of those who 'through faith and patience inherit the promises' (Heb. 6:12), and Caleb is a prime example. He was not over-eager, rushing in; he was not over-anxious, worrying whether it would happen. He knew it would. He had waited patiently through thirty-eight years in the wilderness; he could wait another seven.

But now was the right time, and he stepped forward in faith.

Caleb's challenge

We should not underestimate the challenge he faced. He was proposing to conquer a mountain! We speak of 'climbing mountains' as a metaphor for confronting a challenge. Caleb was not just climbing a mountain, but conquering one! And not just any mountain, but a mountain defended by giants! And all this at the age of eighty-five!

Even climbing a mountain at that age would be a challenge. In 2013 a Japanese mountaineer called Yuichiro Miura climbed Everest (for the third time) at the age of eighty; he hopes to climb it again when he is ninety.[1] But he is very much the exception. Most people at that age prefer just to look at mountains, rather than climb them, let alone go on a military expedition to conquer one!

Conquering any mountain is not easy. Military strategists speak of the advantage of the high ground. From there you can see all around you; you can see the enemy coming, and if they attack, they must do so uphill. It is a task most generals would avoid if they could. Conquering this mountain would have been almost impossible, because of those 'giants' there.

It was, in fact, probably the hardest challenge Caleb could possibly have asked for. And he knew it; he had, after all, seen this mountain before.

He did not have to take on this challenge. Although Caleb speaks of 'this mountain of which the LORD spoke to me' (v. 12), God had promised him 'the land where your foot has trodden' (v. 9). Caleb's foot had trodden all over Israel, so he could have chosen anywhere he wished! No doubt, as he was the 'grand old man' of Israel, they would happily have given him any land he asked for. He could have chosen some fertile valley, or some pleasant city, in an area already conquered and pacified, and settled down to a quiet retirement.

But no—he wanted that mountain! God's promise certainly included that mountain, and Caleb would have it, however difficult it was.

Caleb's faith

Taking on this challenge was a matter of faith. The key word in his demand is 'therefore', linking it to all that he had just said, about the Lord.

Caleb believed God's promise. He knew from experience that God was faithful to his word. God had, after all, brought them out of Egypt, as he had said he would. He had brought them through the wilderness, as he had said he would. He had brought them into Canaan, as he had said he would. If he had promised Caleb 'this mountain', then this mountain would be his.

He believed also in God's power. The same God who had defeated the Egyptians could surely defeat these giants as well. He had believed that forty-five years ago; he believed it still.

He was not relying on his own strength. True, he had just mentioned his strength, but his reasoning was not 'With my strength, I can drive them out', but 'It may be that the Lord (who has kept me alive and given me this strength) will be with me, and I shall be able to drive them out, as the Lord has said.'

The word 'may' there is not a sign of doubt, but of humility. It is similar to what he had said at Kadesh Barnea: 'If the LORD delights in us, then He will bring us into this land' (Num. 14:8). He is trusting in God, believing, as Paul puts it, that 'If God is for us, who can be against us?' (Rom. 8:31).

The strength God had given him would help—indeed, it may be that God had given him this strength for this very purpose—but strength alone is not enough. The strongest man might have failed to take that mountain. But the eternal God, who had promised him that mountain, would give him the victory. With God's help, it was possible—indeed, with God's help it was certain.

This was Caleb's faith: a rock-solid faith that had stood the test of time. He had said, in verse 11, that his strength was the same as it was forty-five years before; his faith was the same also: an unchanging faith in the unchanging God.

With that faith, he was ready to take on the challenge—ready to go into battle, ready to risk his life, willing to stake all on the promise of God; he was confident that God would not let him down, and that God would fulfil his word.

He was saying to *Joshua*, 'Give me this mountain', but really his heart was saying to *God*, 'Give me this mountain'—and he knew he would do so.

Mountains today

As mentioned earlier, 'mountains' are often used as a metaphor for 'problems'. And there are great promises in the Bible that encourage us to believe that, with God's help, we can overcome every problem, every difficulty, every obstacle in life.

There is, for example, the promise to Zerubbabel, when he was rebuilding the temple: 'Who are you, O great mountain? Before Zerubbabel you shall become a plain' (Zech. 4:7). There was the promise of Jesus, made outside Jerusalem, when the disciples were amazed at the withering of the fig tree: 'Jesus answered and said to them, "Have faith in God. For assuredly, I say to you, whoever says to this mountain, 'Be removed and be cast into the sea,' and does not doubt in his heart, but believes that those things he says will be done, he will have whatever he says"' (Mark 11:22–23).

The lesson of Caleb, though similar to this, is not quite the same.

Caleb did not want 'this mountain' removed; he wanted it exactly where it was—but he wanted it to be his! 'This mountain' was his inheritance, and he wanted to claim it for himself, and take it away from those giants.

The equivalent for us, therefore, is not overcoming problems, but rising to the challenge of Christian work.

We can apply it to missionary work. Dr Helen Roseveare, a missionary doctor in the Belgian Congo in the 1950s and 1960s, entitled her autobiography *Give Me This Mountain*. The challenge of world mission is huge. Jesus said to his disciples: 'All authority has been given to Me in heaven and on earth. Go therefore and make disciples of all the nations …' (Matt. 28:18–19). The key to that also is the word 'therefore'. Because all authority is given to the risen Christ, we can and we must make disciples of all nations. God says to his Son in Psalm 2, 'Ask of Me, and I will give You the nations for Your inheritance' (v. 8). Every missionary is seeking to conquer some 'mountain', to take some country, town or village away from that worst of all 'giants', the devil, and bring it into the kingdom of Christ, as his inheritance.

And missionaries often face enormous difficulties in doing so, learning the local language, adapting to the local culture, overcoming local resistance and sometimes even facing persecution.

We can apply it equally to local church mission. Taking the gospel to some nearby housing estate can be just as much a spiritual mountain as overseas mission. Winning the lost is never easy, wherever they are. We face our own mountains and our own giants, in every part of the world.

We can apply it to any aspect of church work. For some, becoming a pastor, an elder or a deacon might be the great challenge; for others, starting, or taking over, a church youth group; for others, taking on the church accounts! We might say of any of these tasks, 'Give me this mountain!'

We can even apply it personally. Laying hold of our own 'spiritual inheritance' is no easy task and could be thought of as conquering a great mountain. It is only possible through faith in God.

The question is, who will take on these challenges?

It does not appear that anyone else volunteered to take on Caleb's mountain. Perhaps—to give them the benefit of the doubt—they all knew that Caleb had set his heart on it and that God had given it to him, and they did not want to interfere with that. But there was certainly no queue of would-be conquerors asking to take on that particular challenge.

And that is the common experience in churches. There may be some tasks which everyone enjoys and everyone is willing to get involved with, but in every church there are certain tasks which no one seems to want to take on. Where are the Calebs, full of faith, full of courage, full of enthusiasm, stepping forward to take on the difficult tasks that no one else wants?

Certainly church leaders should be willing to take on the 'mountain' tasks, setting an example to the congregation. Caleb set an example as a leader in Israel. He was not content to command from the rear, sitting in his tent, allowing other men to fight for him. He was willing and eager to lead from the front. 'Give *me* this mountain,' he said—not 'Give it to my men and *they* will conquer it for me', though I am sure they were capable of doing so. Others, no doubt, would help him—he would not have to conquer 'this mountain' alone. But he saw it as *his* challenge: 'Give *me* this mountain.' What an inspiration to others!

His age made him even more of an inspiration. Israel's most venerable elder was showing them the way. If an eighty-five-year-old could conquer a mountain, what could the younger men do?

How we need men (and women) who will set an example like this today—leaders who will lead, Christians (young and old) who will demonstrate faith in action, role models we can look up to and follow—like Caleb!

Mission accomplished

Joshua, naturally, granted Caleb his request. How could he not? 'And Joshua blessed him, and gave Hebron to Caleb the son of Jephunneh as an inheritance. Hebron therefore became the inheritance of Caleb ... because he wholly followed the LORD God of Israel' (Josh. 14:13–14).

And Caleb conquered his mountain. This is implied in Joshua 14, where, having explained that Hebron used to be called Kirjath Arba (Arba being the greatest of the Anakim), it ends by saying, 'Then the land had rest from war' (v. 15).

It is confirmed in chapter 15, which describes the inheritance of Judah. Having repeated that Joshua gave Hebron to Caleb (v. 13), the passage adds, 'Caleb drove out the three sons of Anak from there: Sheshai, Ahiman, and Talmai, the children of Anak' (v. 14).

The sequence of events is actually quite confusing. Reading Joshua 10 and 11, you get the impression that Joshua had already conquered Hebron and the surrounding countryside, and had driven out the Anakim:

So Joshua went up ... and all Israel with him, to Hebron; and they fought against it.

And they took it and struck it with the edge of the sword—its king, all its cities, and all the people who were in it; he left none remaining. (Josh. 10:36–37)

And at that time Joshua came and cut off the Anakim from the mountains: from Hebron, from Debir, from Anab, from all the mountains of Judah, and from all the mountains of Israel; Joshua utterly destroyed them with their cities. None of the Anakim were left in the land of the children of Israel; they remained only in Gaza, in Gath, and in Ashdod.

So Joshua took the whole land, according to all that the LORD had said to Moses; and Joshua gave it as an inheritance to Israel according to their divisions by their tribes. Then the land rested from war. (11:21–23)

And yet chapter 13 clearly says there was 'much land yet to be possessed' (v. 1), and chapter 15 says that Caleb drove out the Anakim (v. 14).

Some commentators suppose that there were repeated conquests: that Joshua had driven out the Anakim, but they came back. More likely, the closing verses of chapter 11 are a summary of the conquest of Canaan, before 'backtracking' to the allocation of the land and Caleb's request, Joshua being credited with all these victories as the supreme commander.

It seems highly probable also that Joshua would have helped Caleb. Caleb, after all, had helped him; Joshua surely would have helped Caleb.

There is a further difficulty in Judges 1, where the conquest of Hebron appears to take place after the death of Joshua (Judg. 1:1, 10). It is credited here to the tribe of Judah (of which Caleb was the leader), which is actually described as killing the three giants, Sheshai, Ahiman and Talmai (v. 10). Later in the same chapter, when it sums up what each tribe had (or had not) done, it says that Judah gave Hebron to Caleb, and that he then expelled the three sons of Anak (v. 20)—suggesting that they were first expelled by Caleb, and then later killed by his kinsmen.[2]

If all this really did occur after the death of Joshua, it would imply that the final 'mopping-up' operation in Hebron was not completed for many years.

However, it could be that Judges 1 is really giving a retrospect of earlier events—there is certainly a remarkable similarity with the events described in the Book of Joshua. It has been suggested that 'After the death of Joshua' (Judg. 1:1) is a kind of subtitle to the book, and that the opening chapter is a kind of preface.

Either way, Caleb conquered his mountain. His inheritance was finally his—and those 'giants', who had caused so much trouble, were finally gone! How satisfying that must have been! God had fulfilled his word, as he always does.

Caleb could now settle in Hebron—the city where the patriarchs were buried. It later became a 'city of refuge' (Josh. 20:7). It was truly now a place of peace and safety: Caleb's city.

How satisfying it is for us also, when we take on a great challenge and the Lord gives us the victory. The world has a saying 'Fortune favours the brave'. It would be better to say, 'God favours the faithful'.

And we need not be limited to one mountain! There are mountaineers who like to collect 'Munros', climbing all the mountains of over three thousand feet in Scotland, just for the challenge. When one mountain is conquered, we can go on to the next one.

Over the centuries, the church has conquered many mountains; may it conquer many more! And may we all be mountain-conquerors ourselves, achieving great things—even 'impossible' things—by faith.

NOTES

1   Barney Henderson, 'Meet Yuichiro Miura, the Man Planning to Conquer Everest at 90', *The Daily Telegraph*, 1 January 2016, http://www.telegraph.co.uk/health-fitness/body/meet-yuichiro-miura-the-man-planning-to-conquer-everest-at-90/.

2   The first-century Jewish historian Josephus says that their bones could still be seen in his day: *Antiquities of the Jews*, Book 5, chapter 2.

The next generation (Josh. 15:15–19; Judg. 1:12–15; 3:9–11)

W e all care about the next generation. Parents especially worry about their children, wanting the very best for them. For Christian parents, one of the greatest joys is to see their children following the Lord—and one of the greatest heartaches is to see them turn away. As John says, 'I have no greater joy than to hear that my children walk in truth' (3 John 4). Even if you have no children, you will still be concerned for nephews and nieces, and for the next generation, growing up around you.

Caleb belonged to a tragic generation who had seen the Lord mightily at work, bringing them out of Egypt, and yet most of whom had turned away from God and had died in the wilderness. What would the next generation be like? Would they learn? Would they trust in the Lord? God had promised that they would come into the land, but what would they do when they got there?

Caleb had several children, and God's promise included them specifically: 'Surely the land where your foot has trodden shall be your inheritance and your *children's forever*' (Josh. 14:9, emphasis added).

In Joshua 15 we are introduced to one of those children, his daughter Achsah, who married Othniel and asked her father for springs of water to go with the land he had given her. The story is repeated in Judges 1.

Three sons are also mentioned in 1 Chronicles 4:15—Iru, Elah and Naam—along with several grandchildren and great-grandchildren: 'The sons of Othniel [and presumably Achsah] were Hathath, and Meonothai, who begot Ophrah … The son of Elah was Kenaz' (1 Chr. 4:13–15).

We also know about other young relatives. Seraiah, Othniel's brother, 'begot Joab the father of Ge Harashim, for they were craftsmen' (1 Chr. 4:14). 'Ge Harashim' means 'Valley of the craftsmen', so presumably this branch of the family were renowned for their practical skills.

Most of these people are just names to us. We do, however, have that precious story about Achsah, which has much to teach us.

Calling young warriors

The story of Achsah and Othniel takes place against a background of war.

Caleb had just taken possession of Hebron and driven out the 'giants', and had now begun a campaign to conquer the surrounding area, including Debir (Josh. 15:15). This city, we are told, was previously called Kirjath Sepher, which means 'City of the Book', and some think it was an important cultural centre. It is later called Kirjath Sannah (v. 49), which means 'City of Learning'.

Caleb did not, however, propose to capture this city himself. He gave an open invitation for some other young warrior to make a name for himself by taking it. And he offered an inducement: 'Caleb said, "He who attacks Kirjath Sepher and takes it, to him I will give Achsah my daughter as wife"' (Josh. 15:16).

It is always good for older 'warriors' to encourage the younger ones. In a Christian context, Paul says: 'The things that you have heard from me among many witnesses, commit these to faithful men who will be able to teach others also' (2 Tim. 2:2)—handing over the baton to the younger generation. He goes on to speak of Timothy as a 'good soldier of Jesus Christ' (v. 3).

Caleb is saying, in effect, 'You have seen how it is done: I have taken Hebron; now who wants to try the next one?' If Caleb alone had led every battle, he would have left behind a generation of weak, inexperienced men who had never won a battle themselves and might be afraid to attempt it. Instead, he was training up a new generation of leaders.

There was no danger. If it all went wrong, he was still there, ready to step in and help. But if it went well—as it did—another commander would have been 'born'.

Likewise in the church, leaders need to learn when to let go. We should be constantly training younger Christians and encouraging them to use their gifts, being willing occasionally, like Caleb, to step aside.

It worked out well with Othniel: he later became the leader of Israel. Amongst our younger people are our future leaders.

This particular challenge, however, came with a special incentive which possibly we might not wish to offer today: his own daughter!

A marriage proposal

This offer of a wife would not have been considered improper in those days. Until quite recently, it was the custom, even in the UK, for a father to 'give' his daughter in marriage—a tradition still preserved in the wedding service: 'Who gives this woman to be married to this man?' Today this implies no more than permission, but in the past, parents were often more proactive. Royal families especially would choose a 'suitable' wife or husband.

In the Bible, Abraham sent his servant to seek out a wife for Isaac. It was an arranged marriage, but not a forced marriage: Rebekah was given the choice, 'Will you go with this man?' (Gen. 24:58), and she chose to go—a beautiful incident sometimes likened to the Christian willingly going with Christ.

Caleb, however, was not choosing a wife for his son here, but a husband for his daughter. And although it might sound as if he was treating her as a commodity, giving her away to whoever wanted her, he was actually making sure that she had a good husband—a courageous man who trusted in the Lord.

A similar offer was made by King Saul to the man who would kill Goliath (1 Sam. 17:25)—he would enrich him, give him his daughter and exempt him from taxes—though he made the offer out of desperation and fear. David, of course, accepted the challenge, slew Goliath and became the king's son-in-law.

Whether Caleb's daughter, Achsah, was considered a great 'prize' for the young men of Israel, we do not know. Jewish tradition says she was very beautiful; the Bible does not say. She may have been the child of Caleb's old age and a young woman of great beauty—or she may have been, shall we say, more mature. We have no idea of her age, except that she must have been under twenty at Kadesh to have survived the wilderness, hence under sixty-five now. From the way the story unfolds, it appears she was very close to her father and a woman of strong character—probably (though it is not stated) a woman of faith. To a godly man, this would count for more than beauty: 'Charm is deceitful and beauty is passing, but a woman who fears the LORD, she shall be praised' (Prov. 31:30).

She was also, of course, her father's daughter! The successful 'candidate' would become son-in-law to one of the greatest men in Israel. We might almost call it a royal marriage—though Caleb would immediately correct us and remind us that the Lord alone is King!

But there was a price: the man had to conquer Kirjath Sepher.

Othniel rises to the challenge

Othniel now stepped forward: 'So Othniel the son of Kenaz, the brother of Caleb, took it; and he gave him Achsah his daughter as wife' (Josh. 15:17).

There is some ambiguity here as to whether it was Kenaz or Othniel who was Caleb's brother. The Talmud says that Othniel was Caleb's younger brother (and has to explain away the implication that Caleb was the son of Kenaz, when it says elsewhere that he was the son of Jephunneh),[1] but it seems more natural to take it that Kenaz was Caleb's brother, making Othniel Caleb's nephew. That would make Othniel and Achsah cousins.

Marriage between cousins was quite acceptable under Levitical law (whereas marrying your uncle, as the Talmud would imply, was not).

As cousins, they would probably have known each other already; Othniel would have known what kind of a wife he was getting, and Achsah would have known her future husband. She was not marrying a complete stranger, and, as far as we can tell, she was quite happy with the arrangement.

Whether Othniel was older or younger than Achsah, we are not told. All we know is that he too must have been under sixty-five, to be in Canaan.

No details are given of the battle, but we can take it that Othniel fought with faith in the Lord, as victory would have been impossible otherwise.

Here was a fine young man, already part of the wider family, but now Caleb's son-in-law. What a wedding that must have been—a wedding and a victory celebration at one and the same time!

A daughter's request and a father's generosity

Achsah is most famous, however, for the land Caleb gave to her.

This part of the Book of Joshua is mainly concerned with the allocation of land, and it is natural, therefore, that it should mention the land Caleb gave to his daughter after her marriage to Othniel. It was unusual in those days for women to inherit land. Daughters could inherit if there were no sons (Num. 27:8), but in this case there were. But if anyone should query it, her descendants could point to their title deeds here, in Scripture.

This is, however, far more than a story about land. Preachers have seen in it some wonderful lessons about prayer.

Let us follow through what happened.

Caleb had already granted Achsah 'land in the South' (Josh. 15:19), perhaps as a dowry. But she wanted more: 'Now it was so, when she came to him, that she persuaded him [Othniel] to ask her father for a field' (15:18). Achsah knew her father! He was not only wealthy, but generous too; he was sure to say yes!

This may have happened as soon as she and Othniel were married, 'when she came to him' for the first time, the bride being brought into her husband's house; or it may have been later, perhaps after seeing the land given to her. The NIV has simply 'one day'. Either way, the wife used her influence and persuaded her husband (or, some translate it, 'moved' or 'urged' him) to make this request.

She did not, however, leave it at that: she went to her father herself. Perhaps Othniel asked her to do this, or perhaps it was her own suggestion, given the bond between father and daughter. The Septuagint (the Greek translation of the Old Testament) says, 'She counselled him, saying, "I will ask of my father a field."' The request, however, was now for 'springs of water': 'So she dismounted from her donkey, and Caleb said to her, "What do you wish?" She answered, "Give me a blessing; since you have given me land in the South, give me also springs of water"' (15:18–19).

Some think the field contained the springs; others think that there were two requests—the field, and the springs, on top of the land she already had. The point was, however, that she needed water. The 'land in the South', literally the Negev, was a dry land, and it would be useless without water.

One writer has described her as 'Achsah the Pushy'; another calls her 'the discontented bride'—though neither is intended as a criticism. She was, in fact, being entirely reasonable. Her father, surely, would not want the newly-wed couple to live in a waterless desert—especially after his own experience in the wilderness. It would also be a cruel joke on Othniel, after all his heroics at Debir, to give him his daughter with a useless plot of land. Achsah knew her father better than that. He would never do that.

She came respectfully. That probably is the point of her dismounting from her donkey. And she requested it only as a blessing, not as a right. But she was sure he would say yes. Every father wants to bless his daughter!

And she was right. Caleb immediately granted her request—and more: 'He gave her the upper springs and the lower springs' (v. 19). These springs would provide her with an abundant supply of water—all she needed, all she could wish for, to make her land fruitful.

They were *given* to her, notice—a free gift, for which she paid nothing—and they were given to *her*—a father's gift to his daughter.

This says a lot about Caleb. It shows him to have been a loving and generous father, willing to give, to give to his daughter (not just to his sons, as other men in those days might do), and to give even more than she asked for. And that was not surprising; after all, God had been generous to him. God had given *him* an inheritance in Canaan, for himself and his children, and he was happy to share it with his daughter.

Praying to our heavenly Father

It is a beautiful story, but it also contains some profound spiritual lessons. No moral is actually drawn from it in the Bible, but preachers have found it irresistible as a picture of prayer.

We have a loving and generous heavenly Father, far wealthier than Caleb. Heaven and earth are his, and he is able to give us whatever we need.

Those springs of water, also, are a picture of God's blessings, flowing out freely to the people of God, making our lives fruitful. Some have likened the 'upper springs and the lower springs' to heavenly and earthly blessings.

This is the language of the Bible. Psalm 87 says, 'All my springs are in you' (v. 7). The psalmist prays, 'Bring back our captivity, O LORD, as the streams in the South' (Ps. 126:4). Isaiah says, of the Messianic age, 'With joy you will draw water from the wells of salvation' (Isa. 12:3); 'The parched ground shall become a pool, and the thirsty land springs of water'

(35:7); 'I will make the wilderness a pool of water, and the dry land springs of water' (41:18); 'Ho! Everyone who thirsts, come to the waters' (55:1). In Ezekiel's vision, life-giving water flows from under the temple (Ezek. 47:1).

Jesus promised the woman of Samaria, 'Whoever drinks of the water that I shall give him will never thirst. But the water that I shall give him will become in him a fountain of water springing up into everlasting life' (John 4:14). Later he also said, 'If anyone thirsts, let him come to Me and drink. He who believes in Me, as the Scripture has said, out of his heart will flow rivers of living water' (John 7:37–38, referring, John says, to the Spirit). And the great promise of heaven is that the Lamb will lead us to 'living fountains of waters' (Rev. 7:17).

But the Bible teaches us to pray for these blessings. Jesus says: 'If you then, being evil, know how to give good gifts to your children, how much more will your heavenly Father give the Holy Spirit to those who ask Him!' (Luke 11:13)—implying that we must ask.

We need those living waters of the Spirit for the fruit of the Spirit to grow in our lives; otherwise, we become dry and barren. We need the Spirit in the church; or it will become a spiritual desert; and if we have already become dry, we need the living streams of revival.

And only God can give it. Just as Achsah had to ask Caleb for those springs of water—he owned them, and only he could give them to her—so we must ask God for the heavenly blessings we need.

But we can also ask for earthly blessings—whatever we need.

Achsah sets us an example in prayer. If she could come confidently to Caleb and ask for those springs, as a blessing from her father, we too can come confidently to our heavenly Father. We too must metaphorically 'dismount from our donkey', coming reverently to God. But we come as his children, and he will hear our prayers. Jesus himself assures us of that:

Ask, and it will be given to you. (Matt. 7:7)

Whatever you ask in My name, that I will do, that the Father may be glorified in the Son. If you ask anything in My name, I will do it. (John 14:13–14)

Most assuredly, I say to you, whatever you ask the Father in My name He will give you … Ask, and you will receive, that your joy may be full. (John 16:23–24)

God delights to bless his children, and he is very generous. He has shown that supremely in the gift of his Son, and Paul reasons, 'He who did not spare His own Son, but delivered Him up for us all, how shall He not with Him also freely give us all things?' (Rom. 8:32). He is willing to give and give, and he is 'able to do exceedingly abundantly above all that we ask or think' (Eph. 3:20).

The sequel

Caleb is mentioned no more after this.

Othniel, however, went on to become the first judge of Israel. The story is told in Judges 3. After the death of Joshua, and the elders who outlived him, Israel turned away from the Lord, worshipping idols and intermarrying with the remaining Canaanite tribes. God was angry and delivered them into the hand of Cushan-Rishathaim, king of Mesopotamia, for eight years. Then the people cried out to the Lord, and

the LORD raised up a deliverer for [them] … Othniel, the son of Kenaz, Caleb's younger brother. The Spirit of the LORD came upon him, and he judged Israel [that is, ruled them]. He went out to war, and the LORD delivered Cushan-Rishathaim … into his hand … So the land had rest for forty years. Then Othniel the son of Kenaz died. (Judg. 3:9–11)

Caleb, presumably, had died by then, but he would have been proud of his son-in-law, who followed in his illustrious father-in-law's footsteps, remaining faithful at a time of national apostasy and leading Israel to victory at a time when he himself must have been quite old, and then ruling in peace.

Although Caleb never held the highest office in Israel, his son-in-law did. We can reasonably assume that he had his wife's support in this. This godly couple must have been a comfort to Caleb in his old age.

There is a burial cave in Hebron, near to the Tombs of the Patriarchs, traditionally thought to be Othniel's tomb. It is still venerated to this day, though being in the Arab part of the city, it is rarely accessible to Jews. Hundreds, however, visited it at Passover in 2016, under military protection.

Caleb's tomb

There is also a tomb called Caleb's Tomb in the Arab village of Timnat Hares, known in the Bible as Timnath Serah, 'in the mountains of Ephraim', where Joshua was buried (Josh. 24:30). Once again, because of tensions between Jewish visitors and local Arabs, the tombs are open to Jews only four times a year.

The Bible says nothing about Caleb's burial, and it seems rather surprising for the tribal chief of Judah to be buried in the mountains of Ephraim, rather than in his own city of Hebron. It is rather appropriate, however, to place these two great men of God together in death, as they were in life.

Caleb's memorial, however, is not a mere tomb. Wherever his bones are, he will be raised up again on the Last Day! His real memorial is his life, recorded in the Bible, for us to learn from and imitate.

Although outshone by Joshua, he should not be forgotten, but remembered always as a man of faith who followed God fully.

May we all be like him.

NOTES

1   Babylonian Talmud Sotah 11b.